Private Lessons

Other Writings by Lillian DeWaters

All Things Are Yours • The Atomic Age
The Christ Within • The Finished Kingdom
Gems • God Is All
The Great Answer • Greater Works
I AM THAT I AM • In His Name
The Kingdom Within • Light
Light of the Eternal • Loving Your Problem
The Narrow Way • The One
Our Sufficient Guide • Our Victory
The Price of Glory
Science of Ascension • The Seamless Robe
The Time Is At Hand • The Understanding Series
The Voice of Revelation
Who Am I • Word Made Flesh

Available through:
Mystics of the World
Eliot, Maine
www.mysticsoftheworld.com

Private Lessons

Lillian DeWaters

PRIVATE LESSONS

First Mystics of the World Edition 2014
Published by Mystics of the World
ISBN-13: 978-0692243824
ISBN-10: 0692243828
Title ID: 4868485

For information contact:
Mystics of the World
Eliot, Maine
www.mysticsoftheworld.com

Cover graphics by Margra Muirhead
Printed by CreateSpace
Available from Mystics of the World and Amazon.com

DeWaters, Lillian, 1883 – 1964
Originally published in booklets:
    The Astonishing New Revelation 1939
    God and Oneself 1950
    The Practice of Reality 1950
    Spiritual Consciousness (unknown)
    True Identification (unknown)
Lillian DeWaters Publications
Stamford, Connecticut

Contents

The facts which Jesus taught about himself must be the facts which we are to see as true of ourselves, else of what advantage would they be to us?

The Astonishing New Revelation

No doubt every single one of us has regarded our relation to the truth as similar to that of mathematics; that is, we have accepted our spiritual position to be that of a student of truth and have used "the science of true thought" to work out our earthly problems.

Some of us are studying Christian Science, some Unity, some the Absolute, and some metaphysics under various other titles; nevertheless, all of us have considered ourselves students of the truth, have we not?

But anon the vision lifts, the scene changes, and a sudden moment's revelation and insight completely rearranges and shifts our viewpoint. We then let go altogether that classification of ourselves as students of truth using truth to solve our problems, and furthermore, we see that as such we have many times felt a restriction or responsibility placed upon us, though we may not have admitted this even to ourselves. Suppose, for instance, we seemed not to have had a sufficient understanding of the truth to make a certain demonstration. Suppose, as students of truth, we could not, at the moment, see clearly or fully enough the nothingness of the seeming difficulty. We might try hard and be earnest and sincere in our endeavors, yet something might seem to weigh us down or prevent a clear insight of the allness of Perfection and the nothingness of the seeming problem. We would persevere of course, and we would continue our search for more knowledge and fuller ability to demonstrate it, but seemingly the demands might appear greater, and the problems seem never to cease. Oh, for that peace where we might sit and rest, as it were, with no thought of an existing problem! Have we not all entertained such thoughts and feelings? To be sure, we have.

Well, now, accepting a certain new insight, we may do this very thing, that is, have no consciousness of an existing problem: for a definitely new vision creates a radical change in our position in this triangle of truth, student, and problem—a most radical change!

Before telling about this astonishing new revelation, let us look with precision to see just how we have been placing ourselves in our relation to truth when practicing Christian healing. Having found that all the discordant pictures of disease and limitations are caused by the false conceptions or erring convictions of mankind, we were then able to see that such pictures had no substance, no power nor intelligence whatsoever, thus, no presence. Stripping such theories of their disguise or pretense of truth, they became absolutely harmless to us, for we saw there was no harm in them; and this resulted in what is commonly called "healing"; that is, the discordant condition ceased, and the harmonious and natural state was again in evidence. Such demonstrations were based upon our awareness and understanding of the allness of God and the nothingness of false beliefs and false conditions. Placing ourselves as students of truth, we practiced our highest vision and understanding of the truth, and this brought about the healing. Is this not so?

But supposing there came a problem to our attention or a condition in our experience which, for the time being, we could not seem to surmount or cause to be dissolved? Suppose that no matter how clear was our consciousness of the facts of life and the unreality and nothingness of false beliefs and false conditions, still the perfect answer did not become visibly present to us. We would wonder what else to do, would we not?

Well, one day while in deep meditation, it suddenly dawned upon me that being a student of truth was not, after all, an absolutely assured or infallible state. One might, apparently, practice all he knew of truth and still the problem remain unsolved. Surely such a position as this could not satisfy me; I saw before me the eternal triangle—the truth, the student of truth, and the problem.

For instance, since both students and problems undergo a continual change, what was certain or sure about the mathematical "triangle," I asked myself, "except mathematics itself?"

As this question forced itself upon me, desperately my heart cried out, Oh, to be mathematics! To be that certain, sure mathematics, with never a question of uncertainty or doubt, nor any necessity to yearn for knowledge! Instantly there followed a moment of blinding light with its electrifying transfusion. It was sudden and swift. As though a curtain had been raised admitting some startling new sight, I saw the indisputable fact with vivid, clear distinctness. I saw that I was mathematics! I was not someone solving problems by applying mathematics, but I was mathematics itself! I was the principles, the laws and rules, and I was not a student at all!

Then under this blazing flood of revelation, what else could I do but exclaim further: Why, this means that I am Truth Itself! I am Life Itself! I am not the student earnestly, ardently trying to see through dream and dreamers, but I am that certain, sure, absolute and changeless Truth Itself! The simplicity of it all amazed and overwhelmed me. Here in this brief but thrilling instant of pure revelation, I saw what years of study and research had never given me.

Of course, I then understood Jesus' dynamic statement, "I am the Truth." Yes, this was it. I was not a student of truth endeavoring to obtain and attain certain states of consciousness, always letting go one for another higher up in the scale. No, I was not this at all—I was the Truth Itself! I was literally the Changeless and Unchangeable, the Perfect and Absolute! What more could I ask? What more could be desired? Did Truth, or true Being, have any association with a problem? Certainly not. Neither, then, did I! "I am the Truth Itself," again and again I told myself in my newly found changed relationship. I am not trying to do, to think, or to know something, but I am the Truth Itself! I am doing, feeling, being the Truth, the Life, and the Way! Oh, the blessed wonder of the light.

Now, once having seen and taken this position, every other thought seemed immediately to fade out of consciousness. while beautiful illustrations and verifications in Jesus' life and teaching came flooding my rapturous thought. How plainly now to see that Jesus never said that he was a student of Life, but insisted, "I am the Life." Yes, this was it—he was not a follower of some particular way, for "I am the Way," he announced again and again. Nor did he teach others how to get rid of darkness, but only emphasized to them, "I am the Light." Indeed, Jesus did not ever speak nor act as though he were using Truth or Life as a means to bring about certain healing results. No wonder he was so absolute, so compellingly certain and sure!

His attention was not toward conditions, dreams nor dreamers, states nor beliefs, but was upon that Nature which is unalterable, that Principle which is fixed and absolute, that Life which expresses continuous harmony and wholeness always. Against such the winds and waves of circumstances might beat in vain.

WE ARE THE TRUTH NOT THE STUDENT

Now, we know that since the beginning of time all the mistakes or errors made in computations, or effected in subtractions, additions, multiplications or divisions of numbers, have never weakened, corrupted nor assailed mathematics. Think of it. Mathematics, inclusive of all its principles, its rules, laws and questions, still remains changeless, despite the sum total of all mistakes made in the solution of mathematical problems and despite all the people everywhere who have made such mistakes. Thus we are convinced that mathematics and all that it constitutes is incorruptible, unassailable, absolute, eternally fixed and changeless.

What difference to mathematics that every day millions of people write down falsities about it? What difference if the whole world agrees upon some computation which is absolutely contrary to its existing facts? Mathematics would be undisturbed by any such mental inconsistencies or false beliefs, since nothing of the kind could ever affect its established from-the-beginning verity, reality or existence.

As one may well be certain of mathematics as being changeless, absolute and unassailable, so sure was Jesus of himself as the Way, the Light, and the Truth—invincible, inviolable, infallible, absolute, complete. And most certainly Jesus' life on earth was to teach us this same fact about ourselves, was it not? All else may change and vary, but true Being, or Truth, remains ever the same. It holds Itself invincible, infallible, indissoluble, true and absolute, always.

Jesus knew that he was the Truth Itself, the Life Itself, the Way Itself, and he said so. He took this position as the fact about himself; thus nothing could ever hurt him, affect or destroy him. Let people think they could throw stones at him. Suddenly they did not even see him, for he had vanished! Let them think they could catch and take hold of him. They found themselves grasping at thin air! Let them imagine they could kill him or deprive him of life and its action, and soon they saw the selfsame being walking in their midst, partaking of food and drink as before, enacting Truth and Life as though not a thing had happened! Jesus not only knew the nothingness of lies and liars, of dreams and dreamers, but he also knew the absolute position of himself. He knew that no dreams of people could affect him—no matter what their dreams! He knew that no beliefs or ignorance, even if accepted by the whole human race for millions of years, could ever interfere with him, since he was immaculate Being; he was changeless and immortal Life; and his body was his consciousness of this reality!

"I am the Truth!" he challenged, "I am the Life! I am the Light! The gates of hell shall not prevail against me." No wonder no evil could touch him nor any harm come nigh him, for he knew the nature and substance of his being, and he relied upon that and upon that only.

Dear Friends, no doubt the great majority of us have often stated facts which we believed were true and thought that we understood them. Then one day, right out of a clear sky, as it were, we really did see them, and we beheld them as we never had before. In fact, we seemed to be seeing them for the very first time.

Yes, it takes the flash of light to open their real meaning to us. It is as though we had been carrying around some beautifully colored and artistically designed box and were satisfied with the mere box itself until, one day, the lid fell off, and there before our astonished gaze lay its real and valuable contents. Thus it is with the beautiful and wonderful statements of truth which we carry about in our consciousness until, one day, the veil lifts, and there in a blaze of light is exposed their real and inner meaning.

All of us have thought and talked about the truth, the student, and the problem. We knew that problems continually vary and change, come and go; we knew, too, that the one called student is very likely to be changing his state of consciousness often, gaining new ideas and letting go former ones. Yet all the while we were accepting the truth to be unchangeable, fixed and certain — in fact, those were the very qualities we were trying to bring about in ourselves. How could we ever have expected to reach the height of changeless Being, since nothing but the Truth is changeless and perfect? Thus, for us ever to be perfect, changeless, invulnerable and incorruptible, *we must be the Truth and nothing less.* When we reach this insight, we know, "It is so."

True, we may have many times used the statement, "I am the Truth," but we used it as a statement only and were all the while considering ourselves students of the truth. Students must look at problems and "handle" them in order to surmount or overcome them. A student may feel that since evil of every kind is actually untrue and unreal, he cannot therefore be harmed by it. But when one is touched by the Jesus-Christ-light, he sees that truth is not proven true because of the nothingness of evil, but truth is true because of the nature of itself. Truth is what it is, and it is unchangeable perfection always.

So now, when attempting to "demonstrate" for ourselves, we may take our vision away from all seeming discomfort or discord and instead observe and understand our nature to be as fixed and as immovable as any principle of mathematics. Then we need no longer consider dreams nor dreamers; beliefs, thoughts nor believers. Seeing our being as it really is, we will have no idea of needing a treatment. Nor will we feel the presence of a problem.

This new light will answer many questions for us, questions which we have been, so far, unable to set aside. We may have been wondering why it is that despite our good endeavors, our clear understanding and deep feeling, nevertheless a so-called trouble seems to persist. The answer is that we should take another step forward: we should let go all anxiety or concern about the problem in the contemplation, joy and grandeur of Ourself as the Truth—the Being of changeless perfection and immovable nature and the Principle which is inevitable, certain and fixed. "I am the Truth, and not a student of truth," we may now acclaim, "and as such I am established in perfection and completeness, to which nothing can be added nor taken away." Seeing and feeling this completely, we will have no desire or thought for any other form of prayer or treatment.

Mathematics proves the nothingness of erring beliefs and mistakes about it by always remaining fixed and absolute in its principles, rules and statements. Jesus proved the nothingness of ignorant or helpless mind and of sick or dead life by knowing the nature of Mind or Life to be nothing less than such Principle and Being which is "without shadow of turning," and which is established as perfection and completeness, without variableness, throughout eternity.

Therefore, do not see the one you are helping as young, old, relative, friend nor stranger; neither as ignorant nor yet as a student of truth. But see the one you wish to help as the very Truth, as the compound and composite Principle, including all the laws and expressions of Being, and as that very Mind and Life which is "without blemish and without spot."

It is absolutely certain that Jesus never taught he was a disciple or student of truth but that he was the Truth Itself. If you can't see the tremendous distinction between these two positions, then for illustration, look at the great gulf fixed between mathematics and the student who is applying it. Surely you can see the great difference! The student-position is often one of strife and struggle, mutation and evolution. Jesus promised that the truth-position would set us free from all such labor and contention. He never said nor intimated that he was endeavoring to find a certain way or path which would take him out of difficulties and lead him into health and happiness, but stated with unquestionable authority, "I am the Way; I am the Way Itself; I am the Way here and now!" He did not teach that he was presenting a beautiful, glorious light which, if others followed, would bring them into eternal life, but stressed, "I am the Way, I am the Light, I am the Door." Now, dear Friends, if Jesus is our absolutely perfect teacher, then it is certain that we shall ultimately arrive at this very understanding which he had, and so make the same claims and assertions.

As the Truth We Never Sinned

As true Being, we have never been limited in any way. We have never been born; never suffered sickness, sin, nor sorrow; never made a mistake nor entertained a false belief. For does mathematics know anything about erring computations, or light know aught of darkness?

But as students of truth, we certainly did entertain many false beliefs. For instance, that we left our Father's kingdom, our perfect state of being. Also, we believed that we were sick and were healed; were ignorant and received instruction; were sinful and were forgiven. But we now see that as the Truth, we have done none of these things! As the Truth, or divine Principle, we never had a false belief; never were sick nor imagined ourselves so; never sinned in any way; and never left our state of being the Truth; even as no mistake ever entered into mathematics nor could any error mingle with it.

As the Truth Itself, we can truthfully and honestly say, "I am whole; I am complete; I am changeless and absolute Perfection always." But never as the student can we speak with such absoluteness. Oh, what a difference it makes to us in our visions and expressions—to be the Truth and the Life rather than the student applying the truth to his problems! And so long as one considers himself a student, will he find himself confronted with problems. For are not problems part of the life of a student?

To be the Truth is to let go automatically of the lesser visions and misconceptions. Here I "lose" my life as a student or disciple to "find" it as the veritable Life itself, the Principle "without shadow of turning." Now I can no longer call myself an "idea of God," or a "manifestation of Life," nor will I strive after right thinking. As the Truth, I will *be* the divine Mind and so perceive and know reality and perfection. Only as the one Consciousness can I ever hope to feel imperishable Life, all-adoring Love and unspeakable peace and glory. Only as Life can I ever be immortal, incorruptible and everlasting.

"I ascend unto my Father and your Father, and to my God and your God," explained Jesus. He ceased operating as the Son when he saw, "I and my Father are one; when you see me you see

19

the Father." The Jews said to him, "Thou makest thyself God." Yes, he did this very thing, and he further admonished, "Follow me; the works that I do shall you do also," when you see as I see, think as I think, speak as I speak, make yourself God as I do; for we are all the same One. As I am the Light, so you are this same Light; as I am the Truth, the Life, and the Way, so, likewise, you are the same. We are all the selfsame One and there is no other.

When we see this truth for ourselves we may also transmit it to another who is willing to receive it. We will both be carried away with the glory of being the absolutely fixed, changeless and perfect Truth Itself. We then shall prove that true Being cannot lack anything, cannot be other than what It eternally is. We shall feel for a certainty that Life is always harmonious and so is ever harmoniously expressing Its glorious and luminous Being. Thus our treatment or prayer will consist of words of authority and power, words of recognition and praise.

Our Father which art in heaven—our real and perfect state which awaits our recognition and acceptance of it; *Hallowed be thy name*—only and glorious One. *Thy kingdom come,*—that is, this almighty knowledge is within reach of us all, and in proportion to our readiness and willingness to receive it, so shall we possess it. We do the *will* of God when we see that we are Life, Truth and Love, and nothing less. *Our daily bread,* or spiritual substance, is our daily awareness and acceptance of our real name and nature. This reality feeds, sustains and preserves us with life all-harmonious and ever-lasting. Our "sins" are all blotted out and forgiven on the basis that we are changeless Principle, and as such, we never knew sin, sickness nor grief, nor even false beliefs. We never were alienated from our all-perfect Being. This divine understanding, received and felt in our hearts, *delivers us from all evil,* and we rest secure in the exalted awareness that to be perfect we must be Perfection—we must be perfect Life, Truth and Love, for only such is *the kingdom and the power and the glory forever.*

Verily, until we actually see and feel that we are the Truth, and not the student of the truth, we shall ever be trying to get ourselves out of difficulties called problems. Only when we see that, "I am the very Truth Itself, I am the very Life Itself," shall we have no thought of a problem, even as to light there is no darkness whatsoever. To the Truth all is perfection, and to the divine Mind all is understanding, always.

Our beliefs change, our thoughts change, our ideas and perceptions change, but Truth changes never. Thus, until one discovers that he is the changeless Truth, he is bound to climb and fall, and to climb and fall time and time again. Only when he reaches the knowledge that he is the Truth and so begins to make himself as God, does he enter into that peace where there is no urge to resist evil in some fashion; no desire to handle appearances in any way, for there is the conscious experiencing of the Light, the drinking from the living waters from which he shall never thirst again.

Now, one is always the Truth despite any beliefs or appearances to the contrary; but until he awakens to this fact and partakes of its glory, he does not consciously experience this reality of himself.

The Instruction of Jesus

Awareness of his God-Being lifts one into the experience of his true position. Here he enjoys harmony, peace and plenty. He looks out upon the perfect manifestation. He loves to "speak with authority" and to deal with perfect Being only. He does not concern himself with false appearances, for he is aware of the changeless Perfection and he lives in that consciousness. Enjoying the experience of health, wealth and happiness, he is satisfied and at peace. To be sure, he earnestly desires to hold steadfast to this vision and to constantly enlarge upon it by magnifying and praising it.

So, dear Friend, you, too, are going to experience perfect health and activity, unlimited freedom and the abundance of all good, but not because you will destroy false beliefs or set aside manmade laws and calculations. You are going to experience health, wealth and happiness, but not because of any destruction taking place anywhere, nor because of any right thoughts or beliefs which, as such, you will add to you, but only because you are the Truth and nothing but the Truth! You are Life immortal and incorruptible, and you have never been otherwise! You are that Light which knows no darkness, that Being which claims, "I am the Way, the Truth, the Life; I and my Father are one."

When you recognize that this is the teaching of Jesus, you will willingly and gladly accept it. And when your desire is to put aside all other teachings which do not agree with this divine instruction, you will speedily understand it. As your heart speaks to you, follow it; and if your heart does not speak to you, then make room for this glorious event to take place by curbing all mental efforts to "handle" appearances and giving yourself whole-heartedly to God. This act alone will bring a certain glow and warmth to you and a feeling of loving comfort and cheer. Soon you will begin to feel a soft, gentle peace stealing over you, for you are allowing the instruction of Jesus to penetrate into the very depths of your being.

"Thou maketh thyself God" (John 10:33). So in order that we follow Jesus and embody his teachings and precepts, we must make our life the God-life, our mind the God-mind, our body the God-body, ourself the Truth and the Way, even as he did; we must also turn from lesser visions.

This should not be done in an intellectual way, but with the heart only. The way of the heart is also the way of true understanding, for where your heart is, is your enlightenment also. Jesus said of himself, "I am the Truth," while our present-day teachings regarding ourselves are to the contrary, for we have been taught to believe that we are not the Truth but man, the student. The discerning Paul says of Jesus: "Who, being the form of God, thought it not robbery to be equal with God. Thus we are admonished to do all things "in his name," in the name of the Truth, the Life, the Way. "Know ye not your own selves, how that Jesus Christ (the Truth, the Life, the Way) is in you, except ye be reprobates?" — backsliders, refusing to see or acknowledge the real truth about yourselves!

When we are willing to take the position Jesus took, disregarding former beliefs that we are "ideas" of Truth or "manifestations" of Life, we will be more completely embodying the instruction of Jesus. It is, of course, of no personal credit that we are the Truth—far from it! We are the Truth only because it is our nature. Yea, from everlasting to everlasting we are the Way, the Truth, the Life, and all opposing thinking or believing can never change us.

"Search the Scriptures," for in them is contained meat for the adult as well as milk for the babe of the Word. As we move forward and ascend, gradually the scales fall from our eyes and a new vision appears. Finally there comes the immaculate conception—the recognition and realization that, "Ye be therefore perfect," for as I am the Light, so you are the Light; as I am the Truth, so you are the Truth; and as I and my Father are one, so you and your Father are one.

Inevitably, therefore, all lesser visions and beliefs must finally be renounced, for we are destined to know ourselves as Jesus knew himself; nor can such destiny be put aside. The boy is not destroyed when he becomes a man, nor the son when he becomes a father, yet definitely a new life begins, also new visions, hopes and experiences.

"I come to fulfill," proclaimed Jesus: I come to fulfill your destiny and bring to you the conscious awareness and knowledge of your eternal state. As you accept my teaching and follow me, you are bound to enter into the resplendent light of your own Being. In this realm of pure revelation, one simply enjoys, without thought or struggle, the things which are his as the Truth and the Life—the things "prepared" for us all from the foundation of the world.

The Old and the New

We gave up the material methods of healing disease when we entered the plane of taking thought. We gave up the mental system of healing disease when we entered the plane of spiritual consciousness, that place where, as students of the Absolute, we beheld the allness of reality and the nothingness of opposing beliefs. But when we reach that exalted and growing awareness that we are the Truth and not the student, then we practice in a new way. Light does not know that it is removing darkness, for to light there is no darkness whatsoever. "Ye must be born again" and again, ever and ever, until that day when pure revelation dawns, and you know that as the Truth you were never born and never have been other than the Truth—that very Being which is change-less perfection, always.

When you make a statement *about* the Truth, it is not the same as when you speak *as* the Truth. When you deal with the nothingness of evil, it is not the same as when you *know* the inviolable and undefilable nature of yourself as the Truth. When you consider your body as following the dictates of your right thinking, it is not the same as when you are absent from all thought of the body and present with the Lord—the Light which illuminates you and your world.

You shall know the truth that *you are the Truth*, and such knowledge shall set you free from ignorance and darkness. When we know this Truth in part, then we shall be set free in part; but when we know this Truth in full, then we shall completely experience that Perfection which has always been our genuine Being.

To turn away from false beliefs has been a great step forward; and to stop being the false believer has been a still further step in advance. Truly to see the absolute nothingness of evil and to bring about the demonstration of such vision in instantaneous deliverance was a great step above the mental system of making thought a healer. But to consider oneself as the Light which knows no darkness, oneself as the Truth without spot or blemish, this insight and knowledge touches the hem of the garment of Jesus' presentation of the true Light and inevitably brings one into the conscious awareness of peace, abundance and harmony as here and now, and of heaven on earth as the present possibility for us all.

THE KINGDOM OF PERFECTION

When we are illuminated by the Spirit, we stand in speechless wonder at the glory within and about us. Our burden of fear, doubt, anxiety and dismay, quite suddenly, completely vanishes. Now we are conscious only of the presence of a soft, ineffably sweet and altogether satisfying peace and contentment; a deep calm and absolute rest.

In this lighted and exalted state of being, we feel as though we were at that instant experiencing the effect of those authoritative majestic words: "Peace, be still." Instantly the inner surge of fear and worry, of inefficiency and helplessness ceases. We have no feeling of having been moved out of the way of the storm nor of being transported to some other realm or place. We are quite aware of the same self, the same body, the same being—but now the storm has ceased, the sun is at its height; indeed, the world is crammed full of glory, while the heart sings and soars; and all the while we are resting in "the everlasting arms" of Life triumphant. With the burst of sunshine through the storm clouds, we know and feel all is well; all is heavenly glory and wonder; all is harmony and completeness; all is perfection everywhere.

When one experiences this enveloping of the light, this comforting and exhilarating state of poise and stillness, of rapture and peace, he knows within himself: Behold, it is finished; *I* am come, the living Christ, the Life triumphant.

"The place whereon thou standest is holy ground." The world wherein we are living is really the kingdom of heaven. The body which we are motivating is actually the body of light and harmony. The being which we call "me" is verily the Life and the Truth. Oh, it is a glorious world, this world which we see as heaven and this body which we know as the temple of the living God, and the consciousness of Life triumphant is surely a state beyond verbal description. Here in the exalted state of being, we are aware only of feeling; we know and accept through feeling only, for such feeling includes knowing. It is all-satisfying and leaves nothing to be desired. It is a full and complete experience. It is the effortless action and laborless motion of the one Life-Mind-Being-God.

Here in this state of reality there is no sense of independence nor of dependence, of striving to know, nor to be still. Here there is no sense of labor whatsoever. We simply enjoy what is taking place; we enter into the experience of that which is prepared for us. We do not think statements of truth; indeed we are not conscious of any effort to think at all. We are conscious only of accepting, of receiving and entering into the one Mind-Life-God.

You ask, "Oh, how can I bring about such an experience in my own life and in myself? How may I leave this experience of misery and turmoil, of lack and limitation, struggle and strife?" Very often after we have experienced this exalted state of being, we are unable to discover what brought it about, for quite suddenly and unexpectedly we walked, as it were, in another world, we partook of another life—and enjoyed a higher freedom. In meditating upon it afterward, we do not recall opening any certain door to this view of the super-world, of doing anything in particular which released the light, nor of walking in any certain direction which terminated in this glorious heaven.

Yes, it is often this way, that when we look back to discover just what took place and where the change began, we are unable to find the precise spot or discover just how the great event happened. It was as if while walking along a dusty, rutty road, framed with briars and weeds, we suddenly found ourselves resting in soft "green pastures," and by "the still waters" of refreshment, beauty and peace! Wiped out of our consciousness were all thoughts of imperfection of any kind. We had no memories of past failures nor present difficulties. We knew only the blessed joy and sweet security of the moment. Now, such a state of consciousness may remain for moments, hours, and even for days and weeks at a time. And it is never possible for one to ever completely forget it.

But to return to the question of how to consciously bring about this exalted state: desire must, no doubt, precede it. Our desire may be for a way out, or for light and revelation, or even for surcease from sorrow, suffering or despair. "Ask," said Jesus, "knock." On another occasion he said, "Open the door, and I will come in." He gave other commands too, such as: "Be ye therefore perfect, even as your Father which is in heaven is perfect." Our attainment or fulfillment of this command simply means our coming into recognition and acceptance of the fact that perfection could never be imperfection: it could never be anything less than perfection every instant and in every place. Thus the kingdom which is prepared and at hand must be the kingdom of perfection. Here one is not to work to attain, but is asked only to accept and receive—and to think, feel and see perfection as his own Being.

This kingdom which is prepared and at hand, is it not a place of consciousness and body? Have you not had the exalted experience of directing your attention from imperfect body to perfect reality, thereby concurrently to express harmony and ease? This shows how a state of consciousness, when turned from appearances and false beliefs to the true facts and real state of life, simultaneously expresses itself in bodily form. The body is consciousness and nothing else—verily, the body of consciousness.

Now, this does not mean that our bodies are conscious, for they are not. Our bodies are the reflected or expressed state of our consciousness, and so if our understanding is that we are Life, Soul, Principle and, as such, are as fixed, certain and unchangeable as mathematics, then we will express this consciousness in a well, strong, active and healthy body.

How could we ever hope to express an impalpable body of light, as Jesus portrayed on the mount, while we entertain the belief that it is material and subject to sickness and death? Or how could we ever expect to do away with a form of age and limitation and with feelings of physical discord and sickness while we accept the idea that we have a body which is controlled by a so-called "mortal mind"?

"Be ye therefore perfect" in your thought of your body! Accept your body to be one with your life, and so spiritual, perfect and complete, even as in your life itself; not one with a human mind, but one with you, the divine Mind and Truth. Separating one's body from one's self, that is, considering the body matter and the self Spirit, is the very belief which culminates in the experience called death. No one would believe that a spiritual body could die!

Surely so long as it is accepted that a human mind controls a human body and that the body we now manifest is not spiritual but material, so long will death be apparent; for what is the end of materiality but self-destruction and annihilation? What a change would appear in this world if different ideas were entertained about the body! In order that it be transparent, weightless, and radiant as the light, we must become consciously aware that such a body is the only one there really is; and we must be willing to give up our belief in any other. We have heard it said that, "What thou seest, that thou be-est." Theoretically this is so, and one does experience what he believes; but exceeding this, what you are, *you are,* regardless of any position you may assume. To comprehend this transcending fact will help release you from human bondage.

"Abide in me, and if ye abide in me, ye shall ask what ye will, and it shall be done unto you." Here is a definite, impressive promise from on high. In proportion as we abide in the awareness that the Truth includes both our soul and our body, we shall be standing on the rock of Gibraltar, which no wind or wave of circumstances can move. Here, although the storms may come and dash upon us, we shall be as that "house" about which it is written: "And it fell not: for it was founded upon a rock."

The greatest fact we can learn is the knowledge that we are the Truth; and as we truly come into the positive and luminous awareness of this eternal fact, the lesser views of relationship will completely and effortlessly fade away. One could think of no greater art than to speak as the Truth, to speak authoritatively.

Our Divine Qualities—Ever present

Nearly all the branches of spiritual metaphysics stress the necessity of becoming more spiritually minded and more active in the operation of purity, honesty, goodness and love. Surely this has been a great step forward and away from the belief that one is the victim of heredity, personalities, circumstances, and conditions. Nevertheless, such constructive thinking and learning to be divine shall be overarched and transcended by the awareness of one's innate and inherent qualities of goodness and wholeness. As we stand for what we are, and as the One we are, we shall come to see that being good, being loving, honest and pure, is not a matter of attaching such divine qualities to ourselves, but rather the capacity of operating from the position that as we are the Truth, we are therefore *intrinsically and divinely good and true.*

As one comes into the clear awareness of his divine Being, he simultaneously comes into contact with that state of honesty and goodness which is his own. Thereafter he will practice kindness, goodness, honesty, and all the various divine qualities so essential to one's happiness and well-being, as though he were simply being natural, operating from the basis that his Being could not be otherwise than true to what It is.

One should not seek for health as though he could acquire it by performing certain physical acts, nor by thinking in some prescribed manner. No. Health is Being. Being is health. To be the Truth is to be well and strong. To be Life is to enjoy absolute ease and harmony. To be Love is to be honest, pure and loving: to be happy and glad.

Abide in Me; all things are yours. Abide in the awareness and enlightenment that you are the Truth, and so your very Being is goodness, love and understanding. Praise and glorify your marvelous Self and Being, and worship here, and here alone. Since you are the Truth, then act and think in accordance with It. No longer need you attempt to grow into health, develop into divinity, nor evolve into some higher self; all such practices must now be abandoned.

Our obligation is not to change worlds, change bodies nor characters, but rather to know ourselves as we are; to look neither toward future realities nor back over the past, but to live in the perfect, eternal Now and to make ourselves God, even as Jesus did; to know as he knew that, "I am the Truth; I am the light of the world; I and my Father are one."

THE REAL JESUS CHRIST MESSAGE

As the Truth, or true Being, we were never made subject to a mental sleep nor dream. As the

Truth, we cannot be mesmerized nor tempted to believe other than that we are perfect Life, Truth and Love. When we find a teaching which does not propose to add anything to us nor to subtract anything from us, but teaches us that we are the Truth, then we have heard the real Jesus Christ message. Do you suppose that what was true about Jesus is not true about us? This could not be so, for he definitely stated, "Thou hast loved them as thou hast loved me."

Jesus admonished us to "seek." When one seeks for health, for wealth or for happiness, can it be said that he is seeking truly? Is he not searching for that which he feels he lacks, something which he wishes to have added to him? And if one seeks for knowledge, what would be the knowledge which finally would completely satisfy him? Surely, nothing but the established-from-the-beginning fact that he himself is the Way, the Truth and the Life! The real Jesus Christ teaching must someday be seen and accepted as the only actual one there is or can be. The facts which Jesus taught about himself must be the facts which we are to see as true of ourselves, else of what advantage would they be to us?

We know that millions and millions of people on earth are faithful readers of the Bible, and perhaps the great majority of them desire to follow Jesus' teachings. He prayed, "That they all may be one; as thou, Father, art in me, and I in thee, that they also may be one in us." Now, how could we all be "one" when there are so many conflicting religious beliefs and practices among us? So long as we consider ourselves students of differing forms of religion, we can never be one in thought. Only when we see that *we are the Truth,* the very same as Jesus, can we genuinely lay claim to oneness with each other and unity with God. Surely you can see this for yourself, can you not?

As the Truth Itself, as the one and only Way, and as the Light of the world, we may truly lay claim to oneness with each other. But in no other way! As the Truth, we are the same Being. As the Truth, we all stand on the Rock which is the Christ. We are therefore neither teachers nor students of truth, nor masters.

Inevitably, a new day dawns. The teachings of Jesus shall be accepted as he gave them. They need no embellishment, nor any peculiar or extraordinary translations. Jesus spoke plainly and clearly, but how complicated and confusing man has made his simple teachings!

As "students," we are continually being sinful and in need of forgiveness; continually striving to let go some disorderly tendency and cultivate some better traits; in fact, our state of consciousness is ever fluctuating. Formerly we were taught to deny our failings and failures and to say of a discordant or distressing circumstance, "It never happened." But many find it hard to affirm what they are told is the fact, since to them it does not seem logical. Something in them insists upon looking back and feeling that a certain unhappy event did really happen in their life. But when one shifts his position from student to Truth, he will have no difficulty in asserting what is so, and his heart and mind will agree when he exclaims, "It never happened; no evil has ever entered my Being!"

"Who convinceth Me, (the Truth), of sin?" demanded Jesus. Could a mistake enter into mathematics? Could some darkness find its way into the light? No more could, nor did, a mistake ever enter into you, the Truth. Jesus never taught any system of healing sickness or sin. He taught that he was the Light, and we know that to light there is no darkness whatsoever. Moreover, he demonstrated that he possessed sovereign power and divine authority to speak the Word and have it come to pass; and thus the vital question for us to ask ourselves is this: Am I going to accept Jesus' teachings as he gave them or not?

Reader, have you ever studied the New Testament very carefully, to see for yourself exactly what he said and did at the times he performed his "miracle?" Did he ever pray to God to do the healing work? Not once. Did he speak with innate power, as though he himself were the only authority to be considered in the case? He did; for the people said of him, "Thou makest thyself God."

When Jesus was told that a man was blind, deaf or diseased, do you suppose he believed it? Surely he knew everyone to be the same as himself—changeless Perfection—by virtue of the fact that we are all the same Life and Being. Knowing the person before him to be as himself—the Truth—then, of course, it was a fact that his sight and hearing were part of his changeless Perfection. Thus Jesus commanded: See! Hear! Walk forth strong and well!

The way Jesus regarded himself in his relation to God, or Truth, should be the way for us to consider ourselves, else why call him a Way-shower? Why should Jesus call himself the Truth, the Life, the Alpha and Omega, and we call ourselves images or reflections, ideas, or students of the truth? Why should Jesus claim himself to be the Way, and we [believe] that some particular church, organization, sect or person is the way? He said, "Ye are gods," but we have made ourselves apart from God. Is this not so?

Unless we see ourselves exactly as he saw himself, how do you suppose we shall ever be like him and do the works that he did? Surely these are searching questions we are called upon to answer for ourselves. Jesus never taught that we were perfect man, nor that he was perfect man. He taught only that he was Life and Truth and that we are all one. How long before the religious world, which claims to pattern after him, will open its eyes to this tremendous reality?

When the scales drop from our eyes and we see ourselves as we are, we shall no longer be bound to church, person, creed nor custom. Mrs. Eddy spoke truly when she wrote in her original textbook [*Science and Health,* pp. 166-167] the following:

> We have no need of creeds and church organizations to sustain or explain a demonstrable platform that defines itself in healing the sick, and casting out error.
>
> We have no record that forms of church worship were instituted by our great spiritual teacher, Jesus of Nazareth ... "The time *now is* when they that worship the Father should worship in Spirit, and no longer in Jerusalem, (the wealth and learning) of our temples"; a magnificent edifice is not the sign of Christ's Church.

It has been said that "Man's extremity is God's opportunity." When one ceases to labor or strive, pray or treat as man, an image, dependent upon an outside God, then and there he has made room for the God within him to act and succeed. Of mine own self, as man, I shall never reach the goal; but all power in heaven and earth is given unto me as the Life and Truth! "The Father is greater than I (as a man or person) ... If ye had known me (as I really am) ye should have known my Father also."

How blind we have been! But praise God we may now "see him as he is" and "be like him!" Nor should we hesitate to spread this astonishing new revelation. No longer should we accept or teach that we are anything other than the one Jesus said he was, since Jesus came for no other reason than to tell and show us the truth about ourselves—that we are not "fallen man" but "are gods"—we are all the same Life and Being.

WE SHALL BE SET FREE TODAY

This truth is the very truth which shall set us free today. As man, our days are limited, our power restricted, our life outside our control; but as Truth Itself, Life Itself, the Way Itself, all power is ours—joy, peace, abundance are now all within our reach.

Can any darkness assail the light? Did any darkness overthrow Jesus? Our only real hope for full deliverance from all evil is to be like Jesus, to make ourselves Life instead of an image of Life, Truth instead of an idea of Truth, Power instead of a reflection of Power, and the Way instead of a follower of some particular system, church or personality.

Let us see things intelligently and in their true light. Let us look directly at Jesus' teaching. He never taught that he reflected Life, Mind or Being, did he? He never taught that he was man or image, did he? Then why believe it? Why not believe what he taught, that we are Life, we are Truth, we have "all power," and we can do "all things?" True, the words *image* and *man* do apply to some specific thing, but the "thing" is not us. It is our body. Life and God are synonymous terms; likewise body and man. We (Life, Spirit) create an image and likeness. My body, for instance, imaging me, portrays my thoughts, ideas and feelings. We never see Soul, Life or Spirit, since such is invisible; we see only Its image and likeness. To perceive and intelligently understand these fundamental facts sets us free from agelong ignorance and misunderstanding this very day.

It was in her *original* textbook that Mrs. Eddy, the pioneer of Christian metaphysics, gave this exact same teaching, for here she states:

To know we are Soul and not body is starting right (p. 39). We are Spirit, but knowing this not, we go on to vainly suppose ourself body, and not Soul (p. 225).

Recently this textbook was reprinted in the United States and can now be bought for even less than its original price.

True light can never be completely lost nor hidden from sight. The one Presence is really all there is of you, of me, of everyone. This Presence is the *universal* Being, yet acts individually as well, that is, we are all included in the universal Presence, nevertheless can act, think and feel individually. This is the Truth and Light which, if understood and accepted, will set us free from ignorance and darkness. This Presence exists here and now complete, both universally and individually, and as we know and feel this to be so, we experience it. We should therefore earnestly strive to see this as the fact and cease believing otherwise, for to know ourselves as incorruptible Life and Truth constitutes our way out of any dream of discord or limitation.

"Behold, I make all things new, and the former beliefs are passed away" (Rev. 21:5). Thus that we are the reflection, or body, is but part of the dream which must now leave our consciousness. Pure revelation does not depend upon any person but is available to us all. New books shall be written, new ideas formed, and new teachings continually spring forth. Truly, the real control of experience is to place our vision upon ourself as the Way, the Truth, and the Life; to stand upon what we are, and as the One we are, and let go any contrary and opposing beliefs. In the proportion that we do this, shall we be likened unto the "wise man, who built his house upon a rock ... and the winds blew and beat upon that house; and it fell not."

We need not strive to obtain a sense of health, but rather know that we *are* health. Nor should we ever attempt to spiritualize our "minds," knowing as we now do, that we do not possess any human thinking instrument at all. We should accept only that we are Mind, and as such we have right and true thoughts naturally. When we finish the work we have been given to do, we shall be seen no more after the flesh. Already we are ascending in understanding, but we must prove all things, even as Jesus did; this is the work which we have not yet completed. Jesus Christ was Lord and Master of all things, never serving anything but making everything serve him; and we must do likewise. Indeed the world needs us, and we have much to do.

THE REALM OF REALITY

There is a realm which we may enter, now and here, without moving geographically from where we are, a realm which is not ruled by time nor space, by people, thoughts nor things. In this realm there is perfect health, wholeness, harmony and goodness. Where is the door located? Listen carefully to Jesus' answer: "I am the door." The *I* as Life, Truth and Love, is verily the only door; that is, in proportion as we see and accept that we are the Truth Itself, and that as the Truth we are all *one*, without distinction or separateness, we shall enter into the experience of this realm of Reality.

The admonition to, "Be absent from the body and present with the Lord" is advice well worth our attention and consideration. This means not to think nor speak of our bodies as so many cells, nerves, muscles, blood, bones, organs, etc., for this is the way that the unenlightened view it. We note that Jesus did not talk after any such fashion. Stop separating the body into parts, for the body is one and indivisible. Think of it as imaging Life, God, and Principle. Shadows of reflections are not changed by giving attention to them, but quite the contrary; so attend to the original, to yourself as you *are*. Inasmuch as you possibly can, forget your body completely.

Instead of attempting to practice a mental system of healing disease, we should be seeing and knowing only a body which is without spot or blemish, a body which is "the temple of the living God." We should discard the belief of a body of perishable cells, nerves, muscles, et cetera, and form in our consciousness a body which is as absolute, complete and perfect as Life Itself; for so long as we consider the body to be corruptible, vulnerable and material, will it appear subject to death and dissolution. When we are willing to renounce all wrong beliefs about the body and understand its real and perfect nature, we shall be taking part in the Christ viewpoint and experience.

Really, there is never any body nor any disease to be healed; there is but a consciousness to be set right. Adjusting the latter, the former automatically takes care of itself. In this way we enter the realm of Reality.

POWER IS IN YOU

We understand now why it is that we have the prerogative and initiative to think rightly — because we are Mind; and why we are destined to live forever and ever—because we are Life. We know, too, why we are to work, watch and pray — because it is our nature to be actively aware of perfection, wholeness and harmony always, and to have no conflicting desire.

Today, much is said and written about the power of thought; for instance: "Thoughts are things"; ... "thinking is the mightiest force in the universe." *Now, you should know better than this.* You should remember what Jesus said: "And which of you with taking thought can add to his stature one cubit? If ye be not able to do that thing which is least, why take ye thought for the rest?"

Thoughts do not generate themselves, so why not look to that which creates them? They spring from you, from me, and from every living one. Therefore, thoughts are not the greatest power in the universe—but you and I and every enlightened one. Power is not located in the thinking but in us, since, "All power is given unto me in heaven and in earth." This statement is final and absolute.

Ignorantly placing power in the thought hinders and so temporarily deprives one of knowing the true fact that he is greater, since he is the conceiver of thought. He is Mind and Powerhouse where thoughts are generated. Without Mind there can be no thinking. Knowing this, he places power where it belongs—in himself. As the world wakens to take its attention from the thought to the thinker and there to place the power and glory, greater strides will be made in transforming earth into heaven.

So be sure you regard yourself as superior to your thinking, for your thoughts come and go, while you abide forever. Nor should you give any heed to the notion of transforming human beings into superman. Every living one on earth appears as a human being only because he yields to common consent. We should never allude to ourselves as human beings, mortals, nor mankind; all such beliefs are part of the dream. Like Jesus, we should make ourselves Life, Truth and Light, nor think it robbery to be equal with God.

Success lies within us only because we are Mind, the Thinker. Health abides within us only because we are Life, all-harmonious and complete. Finally, all things are ours only because we are that Being to whom nothing is impossible. True, we have many things yet to learn about the how and the wherefore, but to begin by placing power where it rightfully belongs is the first step toward success. Other steps will follow in their proper sequence.

HOW TO PRODUCE OUR SUPPLY

How shall I produce my supply? This question arises in the heart of nearly everyone today, so let us see if we can discover the true and right answer. First of all, and the most important, you should understand clearly just where your supply comes from and what it is you need. Ask yourself where you are looking for it, and to whom. Are you locating it out in the world—in this place or that? Are you placing it in the hands of certain individuals? Or is it that you are looking to God outside of you and waiting for His cooperation and support?

The fact is, Jesus, our Master, did none of these things, yet he produced whatever he required, and at once. Then would it not be sensible for us to study the life of Jesus and discover for ourselves just why he was so successful and sure? We know that he did not look to any person for supply, nor ever wait for a certain or crucial time or season. Moreover, we do not find him praying to any outside God for anything. We discover, however, that he depended wholly and completely upon himself—that he was absolutely Self-sufficient. But why? And how?

He was Self-sufficient because he knew that he was the Way and the Light unto himself. He depended entirely upon himself as Mind, all-knowing; as Principle, all-sufficing; as Truth, all-supplying; verily, he maketh himself God! He knew he contained all power within himself, for he said so, and he demonstrated it. He knew that he could speak the Word and it would come to pass, and it was so.

Now then, how far short do we come in measuring up to the understanding and standard of Jesus? Could it be that we are not to embody him in this respect? Absolutely no! "Follow me," he commanded. So then, one of the first things required is that we accept our true position; let this same Mind be in us which was also in Christ Jesus and use It to fulfill our needs. How could we expect to produce our supply otherwise?

As a human or mortal being, you cannot claim to have the divine Mind; you cannot spiritualize a human mind; you cannot copy Jesus, nor can you make the proper use of spiritual ideas and idealities. You must take your position as this Mind to be certain and absolute.

Suppose, for instance, you need some particular activity, such as employment or a job; then look to yourself as the Light and the Way; yourself as

Mind, all-sufficient. Have the utmost faith in this "Power within you" to bring about the thing you need and to do it easily, quickly and successfully. Turn away from people, things, seasons, customs and appearances; depend and rely solely and completely, trustingly and understandingly upon yourself as the Way through which your need shall be fulfilled. As heretofore you have placed your trust and faith in God as outside of you, now place this same trust and faith in God within you. You will assuredly gain a feeling of security, power and peace, and you will soon come face to face with the fulfillment of your desire.

We are required to live and act as though we were actually in the kingdom rather than in some bad dream-world or "far country." Here, in the kingdom, it should be easy for us to find the very thing we wish, right at hand; to speak and have it come to pass; to think and see it manifested. But when we regard God at a distance from us, heaven in another place, ourselves as human or mortal beings, our minds as so many separate mentalities in need of spiritualization, our bodies as limited, perishable materiality—is it to be wondered that under these conditions we cannot demonstrate our supply?

So arouse yourselves and leave the tomb of darkness, ignorance and impenetrability. Come into the awareness and knowledge of yourself as you *are*, into the glory and wonder of your own

Being, which is accredited to have dominion over "the world, the flesh, and the devil" and is empowered to accept that state of perfection, harmony and bliss which we all were before the world began.

"Open the door and I will come in." Open your consciousness, Beloved, to admit the astonishing new revelation that you are the changeless Truth, you are the all-knowing Mind, you are the immortal Life, and as such all things are yours. "Be still, and know that I am God." Therefore, do not seek for statements to repeat nor formulas to memorize, but consider your Self as able and willing to reveal whatever you require or stand in need of. Let the Light come forth in you. Let the Word be spoken by you. Let the Mind in you be Self-revealing. Then you will feel the unspeakable love which comes from an all-trusting, enlightened Consciousness.

It is possible for this Mind to bring to pass in Its own experience whatever It can vision. It is therefore wise for us to state the thing we wish, that is, name it, for everything is known by its name. Do not just state, "I am wealth," or "I desire abundance," but hold your vision to that exact or specific thing of which you are in need. There must be no strain or stress about it, for can you imagine the divine Mind as operating in any way other than a natural, easy manner? All nature portrays simplicity, quietness, ease, so when we use force or stress, we are not operating as the divine Mind. As this Mind or Principle, we may outline, of course, and we should endeavor always to think and act in a simple, quiet way, as though it were perfectly natural; for the instant there comes mental force or labor, we know we have left the way of the Christ teaching.

Yes, it requires faith, trust, confidence, good-will and a renunciation of ourselves as man, dependent upon an unknown God or left at the mercy of our own personalities. But earnestness, honesty, sincerity and goodwill inevitably bring their own just reward and rich blessings.

MAKE ALL THINGS NEW

When Jesus was tempted to cast himself from the pinnacle, or to let go his high vision for a lower one, surely this temptation or these wrong inclinations did not spring from his own thinking. No, it was the voice of Satan speaking to him: Satan meaning, specifically, the voice of the unenlightened, or what is termed today, the race consciousness. And you know how Jesus replied to that challenge.

So, dear Friend, do not feel that wrong thoughts come to you from yourself; but always consider yourself as Life, Truth and Love—pure, holy and without guile. In the Apocrypha to the New Testament, we read as follows:

Fear not the devil, for he has no power over you. The devil doth indeed affright men: but his terror is vain. Therefore fear him not, and he will flee from thee ... They that are full of faith resist the devil stoutly, and he departs from them, because he finds no place where to enter into them ... Be not afraid in the least of his threatenings, for they are without force, as the nerves of a dead man ... Work ye the works of God, being mindful both of his commands and his promises, and be assured that he will make them good unto you.

Thus as we allow Jesus, our Master, to teach us through his words and examples, and as we permit the astonishing new revelation to break forth in all its glorious effulgence, we shall be following Jesus into that realm where we experience eternal dawn, and where "there shall be no night there ... and there shall be no more death, neither sorrow nor crying, neither shall there be any more pain: for the former things are passed away. Behold, I make all things new."

God and Oneself

Dear Spiritual Friend:

For us to know God aright, we must know God as God knows Himself. *God knows Himself as the one individual All.*

To be the one infinite All-as-All, God must be spiritual Consciousness, for nothing other than immaculate Consciousness can be infinite: spaceless, placeless, timeless, unchanging and unchangeable—All-knowing, All-seeing, All-being.

Spiritual Consciousness is the consciousness of Spirit, the one and only Mind. God, Spirit, the one Mind, as His own infinite being, life, nature, His own infinite embodiment, His own infinite world without a creation or a beginning—absolute, alone.

Before one can know oneself as he is, one must of necessity know God as God is, because if God is the *One* who is *All,* then only one's knowledge of this infinite *One-All,* is able to reveal unto him the knowledge of oneself as he is. The attempt, therefore, to know oneself before knowing God aright has been a common mistake.

To know the truth of Being—that God is one only Mind, Life and Being—it is imperative that one utterly, entirely and completely cancel his belief that he is a consciousness or mind of his own, to be developed or changed into the one Mind which is God: for no mind other than the one Mind exists; thus, no mind but the one Mind that is God can know God.

Regardless of any and all books and instructions whose basis is that God is dual, that *we* are dual, that the world and all things are both good and evil, never has there been a second being, a second mind or consciousness, a second nature and will, a second world and existence.

Furthermore, there is now and ever remains that of us which can know the truth of God and the truth of ourself from God direct. This sacred place where we come into possession of the knowledge of God, the knowledge of ourself, the world and all things, is called the heart. This particular word — *heart* — designates, specifically, our innermost spiritual conviction and love; verily, the heart is representative of that only which, as our own spiritual Consciousness, is Spirit, God.

Spiritual enlightenment, which is God, reveals that God is not dual, though taught this in the Christian Bible as follows: "… and God separated the light from the darkness;" "Then the Lord said, Behold, the man has become as one of us, knowing good and evil;" "The Lord saw that the wickedness of man was great in the earth and that every imagination of his heart was only evil continually" (Gen. 1:4; 3:22; 6:5-6 New Revised Standard Version).

No repentance, regeneration, resurrection exists in God, the invisible whole. To be at all, we must be the *One* alone.

Believe not in cause and effect. Believe not in two beings, two minds, two worlds and two existences of everything. See! Know! Understand! *God as an infinite, indivisible, total All is one whole.* This One-All is pure, perfect Being, Life, Mind, Consciousness, Individuality, Embodiment and World. There cannot be, therefore, another being, life, mind, consciousness, individuality, embodiment and world besides the One alone. To believe in another would be not only to dishonor God, but also to disown one's very own Self and Being.

Inevitably, the only way to know God is as God knows Himself. How does God know Himself? The answer is this: God knows He is the only One. Until this first principle is seen, acknowledged and accepted—that God knows He is the only One—one has no way of knowing what *is* Truth, and what *is not* Truth.

Secondly, one must know the truth of oneself. How can one be sure? In one way only—by seeing how God knows us. This answer, like the first, the heart reveals as follows: God knows us as Himself. God knows all individuality, embodiment, identities or things as Himself, for Himself is all God knows and all God sees.

Undeniably, then, one must know oneself as God knows him; one must see himself as God sees him. One can learn this sublime truth from God direct, or he can learn it by association with those of clear vision, whose uncompromising spiritual understanding—that God is the One-All and that oneself is this identical One—admits of nothing contrary to it.

The only way to know the truth of all things is the way of the heart, for the heart only is strong and courageous enough to disregard and reject the traditional religious teaching that God is one and we another. With forthright light and understanding, we accept God as our only Consciousness, and our only Consciousness as God. We will not tolerate the teaching of separation and duality.

The answers of the heart are not found in the general teaching, which is that we are persons, personalities or individuals with mind, thought, will and body of our own, and that we must progress and regenerate ourselves so that finally we shall reach perfection. God's word is: *I* am all individuality; *I* am all being; *I* am all embodiment; *I* am all life and all world; there is none besides Me!

There is not a grain of truth, therefore, in the teaching that we, as another besides God, must be developed or changed into the Perfect by a process called regeneration or resurrection, not only in the here and now, but continued in some future time and place called "the beyond," as "probation after death." One cannot be a self, a mind, a being of oneself; one cannot be another besides *the One alone.* God cannot see aught but Himself. God cannot know aught but Himself. Naught but God can ever be.

God *is* Spirit: thus when we know God aright, we are acquainted with Spirit. Spirit is understandable only when we put aside our belief in matter. If we think of light, for instance, it is not darkness that we are concerned with; we do not confuse the two, nor can both be present simultaneously; seeing one, the other is not seen or known. Seeing body as material structure, with size, weight, dimension, subject to change, discord and destruction, the outlook is impure and imperfect. Now, the fact is, Spirit is our substance, and this substance is our only Life, Being, Mind and Body. However, this fact cannot be known while one is accepting matter, mind and man.

To understand Spirit, we must turn our vision and thought upon Spirit, which is undimensional, the only Mind and Consciousness there is. Spirit Itself is all forms—unchanging, perfect, immutable and secure. When the word *formless* is used, it simply means form which is incorporeal, without dimension, and neither subject to change, time or condition, but is purely Spirit or spiritual

Consciousness. I know I am Spirit only, for only Spirit *is.*

Let us state the fact and principle of Being: *Spirit is All, and All is Spirit.* We will see then what comes forth from It. Since God, Spirit, is one Life, Being and Consciousness, I must know then that I am this Life, Mind, Being, Consciousness. Since Spirit is all embodiment, then my only embodiment or form is Spirit—right here and now. Spirit cannot be matter any more than light can be darkness. Matter, then, is not known, seen or felt by me.

The earth is not both flat and round. I am not matter and Spirit. I am Spirit! My mind is Spirit; my life is Spirit: Mind, Life, Body are all the same One—Spirit. Since Spirit is All-Presence, then my entire self, body and world is immutable, incorruptible, pure, perfect Spirit. Nothing besides Spirit can be present. I see Spirit wherever I look, for Spirit is the very thing Spirit sees—Its own formless, infinite, spiritual world. There is nothing I can see outside my Consciousness. My Consciousness is my kingdom of reality, my entire world. All is visible to Spirit, all is known to Spirit. Spirit is ever revealing Itself to us, for Spirit ever knows us as Itself, the one and only Presence.

What is not Spirit is not present, having no existence. I love Spirit; I love to behold Spirit as my own perfect Self, Being, Body and World. I love to know that Spirit knows me as Itself. I love to dwell upon spiritual oneness, spiritual allness, spiritual peace, glory and bliss. I can see and know only the things of Spirit, for to me, only Spirit *is*.

There are not two beings—God and humanity. There are not two existences—Spirit and matter. I am one, not two. Which one am I: Spirit or matter? God or humanity? I know I am Spirit. Spirit, God, knows me as Itself. I know myself as Spirit, God. None of me is me. All of me is Spirit, God. God is the only one I am. I and Spirit are one, but two as one—but one as the only *I* there is.

UNSEPARATED BEING

Let us face, squarely and unhesitatingly, the status or situation of religion as it is today, as more and more it comes into the foreground; and it must continue to do so, until the truth about religion is seen and known spiritually. There is a countless number of religious denominations, sects, cults, creeds and beliefs existing today, leading over devious roads and ways, each hoping to find, at the end, the perfect world or heaven.

Though multifarious and diversified, strange to say, religions take their origin from a common basis and have a common platform as follows: Their creeds and beliefs are unanimously based upon the assumption that we are not the one Being now and the one Mind now. They separate being into God and humanity; they separate existence into a present human existence and a future spiritual existence; they separate Mind into one perfect Mind and multitudinous human minds; they divide time into a past state of human birth, a present state of struggle, development and translation, and a future state of eternity, when we shall have earned, demonstrated or attained perfection. Without the basic belief in sin and separation, there would be neither creed nor doctrine.

Note well this outstanding fact: No religion affirms one Mind only, one World only, one Being only, and one Existence only—the spiritual One—and that we are this very One, right here and now.

The word *religion* is derived from its roots "re" and "ligio," meaning to bind back. Having accepted Being, Mind, World and Existence as separated into two parts—Spirit and humanity—religion then attempts to bind them back again. To this end it selects systems, methods and practices whereby to re-store, re-generate, and re-establish that Oneness and Allness which never has been separated or divided!

Reader, can you not see that the entire framework for the teaching, that we must move out of a material existence into the spiritual and be translated from a human being into the spiritual, is made up wholly of the belief that we are living now in a material world, as human beings? Otherwise, why the concept that we must make an exodus from this world? And why the admonition that we must put off a human mind? Just where is the dwelling place of a human mind, and who is to put it off, if God is the only Mind? The Absolute message states there is one Mind only, and It does not make contradictory statements. If it be the truth that God is our being and our consciousness; if it be the truth that the perfect world is within us; then the teaching that we must develop into our Self and journey to the perfect world is preposterous and fabulous.

Fear not to give up imperfect beliefs. Let them go. Truth and Reality is all that exists, all that can be known, all that can be experienced. Through spiritual realization or revelation alone can we see things in their true light. Since there has not been any separation between God and us, then never have there been two existences, two worlds; thus, no journey, no translation can be taken or made. Being is World, and World is Being. Outer methods lead astray from the inner way of spiritual light. All teaching pertaining to matter, error, mesmerism, counterfeit, unreality, illusion, or personal "I" or being—who is to be changed into perfection, or Spirit, One—is impotent to behold the deep things of God: that no human being or personal mind exists.

Spirit, spiritual Consciousness, or the one Mind, is a world of Its own. It employs no ways or practices of becoming or overcoming. It is unrelated, unconditioned, unbounded—It is Itself the *One All*. One does not come face to face with Spirit until he is known of the Spirit; for of himself, as a man, a person or a personal individual, he is incapable of saving himself: he can do nothing. One must be inspired within—by the Spirit Itself. When one loves the voice of Spirit more than all else, he is then divinely guided and taught of the Spirit. He knows just when this takes place, for the heart tells him. When one gives himself unconditionally to Spirit, then one's whole life takes on a great and glorious new meaning.

A story of the East illustrates this way of the Spirit quite clearly and vividly. Briefly, it is as follows:

A poor woodcutter supported himself and family by selling firewood which he cut from the branches of trees near the edge of a deep forest. His labor was great and toilsome, and his means, meager. One day he met a sage who said to him, "Good man, why do you not go onward into the recesses of the forest? Go farther into the woods." The next day the man remembered this advice and now went deeper into the woods, and here he found sandalwood, which he sold for a much higher price. Later, he remembered that the Sage had said nothing about sandalwood, but he said only to move onward. The next day he came to a silver mine, which made him very rich; but going still farther, he came to a mine of diamonds and precious stones.

Many are toiling for the healing of the body, the development of a human self; others are weary of this constant work, yet know not what else is to be done. The Absolute message—that matter, humanity and personal minds have never existed, for Spirit is our real and only Self—is unfamiliar to them. Moreover, not having heard of the heart and its light, it seems strange to them that one can actually hear the voice of God, or Spirit, and be guided and taught of Spirit into a knowledge never before heard of.

Those who would come face to face with Spirit must leave the surface ways of treating sickness and developing oneself, for never will these ways satisfy the hungry heart. Only pure knowledge of oneself as Spirit can satisfy this longing. Deeper, deeper must one go within. Here, taught of God, the practice, the overcoming and becoming are laid aside—suddenly they have become void of meaning. Spirit is not a way to health, harmony and perfection; Spirit does not show one how to be healed or changed into perfection, for Spirit *is* Mind, and Spirit *is* Body—timeless, changeless, eternal. Spirit knows no matter, mind or humanity. It has one vision—Itself as One: "I am All."

Looking farther, deeper into reality, one may come across these words of the East: "The eye with which we see God must be the same eye with which God is seeing us."

The reason why more do not come into this deeper light and understanding—that Spirit is an infinite, present Self and World—is because they are still believing the teaching that we are man who can be healed, regenerated into Spirit by degrees. Is the way one of work, resurrection, change? No. Such belief is void of truth. While God remains one pure, perfect, changeless whole as Mind, Life, Being, which is Spirit—the one and only I—there will be no way but His way. There has been no sin, no mortal existence, nothing physical, nothing human or mortal. There has been no mind but the one Mind, no being but the one Being, no world but the one World, namely, Spirit, or pure, spiritual Consciousness.

The timeworn, moth-eaten doctrine of sin, separation and translation is crumbling into oblivion, for it is totally unrelated to the eternal, infinite truth that God knows He is the One alone.

When electricity was revealed, it superseded the use of former lighting means. There were those who scoffed at it, continuing on with the light they had, but electricity remained. Some will not want to accept the revelation that the entire world of being, individuality, embodiment and world is an infinitude of Spirit which can be known by those

who, leaving the superficial ways of becoming—
ever looking farther and deeper into Reality Itself—
become precious jewels of Spirit, which ever abide
in the depths of the heart.

No teaching but that of the Absolute declares
the existence of one Mind only, right here and
now: one Self, One Life, one Individuality, one
Embodiment and one World. All other teachings
place perfection and the infinitude of the One in a
future time and other realm—not in the present
here and now. The way of Spirit cannot be found
in any creed, practice or method of religion, for all
their ways teach and accept two of everything—
duality.

A single flash of divine or spiritual light is
comparable to the finding of a most precious
jewel. Nowhere can these jewels of infinite spiritual
light be found except beyond the teaching of
dualism. Here, in the glorious revelation of the
one indivisible, pure and perfect, whole Mind,
Being and World, our spiritual wisdom, glory,
peace, contentment and satisfaction are an enduring
experience. How long shall one contend that there
is another?

Whatever teachings need to be dispensed
with, whatever teachings believe God not to be the
only One, let them be supplanted by what the
heart sees and says as the living truth: verily, God
is the only One! God knows He is the One alone!

Let the heart answer these questions as follows: Did God see evil? Did God see another existence besides His own world? Did God make a mistake, repent of His mistake and grieve because of it? Did God plan redemption and restitution? Did God become less than the total One and All? What world does God intend to redeem—the world of Himself, or another world? Never can we know the truth of God and the truth of oneself until this truth is revealed to us by Spirit.

Now comes the question, "How can I be healed?" Let one first of all ask himself, "What "I" is in need of healing? What mind or body requires changing? Does God know aught besides Himself, if He is the only Mind?" The only way that one can ever know the truth of Being is *as* this Mind. To *be* this Mind, one must trample underfoot the teaching that we are now other minds and bodies living in another world besides God's perfect universe.

"No one can serve two masters: either he will hate the one and love the other, or else he will stand by the one and despise the other—you cannot serve God and mammon" (Matt. 6:24 Moffatt Translation). Ask yourself: Am I believing I have a mind, a will, a choice and a body of my own? Would one think he needs changing unless he were serving a second teaching—that we are living now in a temporal human existence and that man and the universe must be translated back into Spirit? Remember this: God knows He is the only One. God says: "I am God alone" (Isa. 46:8 Moffatt). God knows no second mind to be spiritualized; no second body to emerge into Spirit; no second being to be resurrected, and no other world to be reached after death.

The whole report and structure of duality is based solely upon mammon—mythical, heathenish, fabulous deities and powers. The eternal God is one God—unrelated, timeless, spaceless, alone without a second; unchanging and unchangeable; perfect, pure, almighty, absolute, supreme. An acceptance of the one *I* can take place only when one lays down the belief that he is someone of himself—not the one *I* alone. Who is able to do this? Only those who are strongly devoted to God, who love God above all else, for to them only does God reveal Himself. We must see in our own heart that God is the One alone and that God does not know another. They who see and accept this one God, one I AM, will preach and teach accordingly.

The one *I* knows Its own mind and individuality as Itself and that no other minds or individuals exist. The former teaching, that we are an idea of God, expression or manifestation of God—though in advance of other former teachings—must now give way to fuller revelation. No personal "I" ever existed, nor personal minds or thoughts; nor do any personal lives or "I's" exist to be saved. Is it not only because of the present teaching that we are not yet the one Mind, the one *I*, that the belief in the necessity for healing continues? The whole doctrine of humanity and healing, mortals and regeneration, personal "I's" and resurrection, persists only because of the general teaching of Adam and Eve, serpent, temptation, sin, separation of individuality from God, Satan, devil, evil, tempter, human mind. God never conceived any of these ideas! There has been no second mind, and neither a third mind called "race belief"—a mind representative of humanity who advertises specific afflictions.

All invented ways of passing from matter to Spirit, from man to God, are fraught with contradictions, ending in failure. *I*, the Eternal, stand alone. God is among you only.

GOD ALONE

If one believes he is in need of healing, let him listen to the instruction of the Absolute on this subject. An analogy of the sun and its infinite rays is amazingly explanatory of God and His infinite individualities. How clear and certain, that a ray of the sun is nothing of itself at all; a ray is the sun itself, since the sun is its own infinite rays. The sun is not composed of anything; it does not include anything; it is one identity—sun—throughout. It has infinite rays, but this is only another name for itself. Its rays are itself, the sun. Rays are not of the sun, nor is the sun the self of the rays. The sun acts as one whole. The sun is all.

Were the sun conscious, it would know its rays as itself, and the rays would know the sun as their own being. Nothing of an external can possibly enter into the sun's rays. Their immunity lies in the fact that they are nothing of themselves; they are the all pure sun.

Following this same perception, it is revealed that God is His own infinite individualities. God knows His individualities as Himself; and His individualities know Him as their only being. If one believes that God is not His own infinite individualities, but that one is someone of himself, his attitude is defined in Galatians 6:3, as follows: "If a man thinketh himself to be something, when he is nothing, he deceiveth himself."

It is because one believes he is not in God, the one *I*, but is an "I" of his own, to be healed or changed, that he constantly strives for regeneration, healing or realization. It is utterly impossible for anyone to be what he cannot be. God's individualities are the *only* individualities that have existence. The real truth one cannot know until he is willing to humble himself and give up all belief in oneself as someone besides God. As a ray of the sun is not a ray of itself but is the sun itself, even so, one is not oneself; he is the one Self—God. Until one knows himself as God knows Himself, or God knows him, he must carry on with the "chopping of the firewood," as related in the story of the woodcutter.

If only one will give up the belief in oneself as a material, human, mortal, physical person or individual and be nothing of himself in his own sight, then the light will dawn; he will know God as his only Self; his belief in healing has passed away.

God is the *I* and the *I* is God. There is no he, she, you, me; Mary, John, animal, bird, forest, water, and so on, as such. This is the *I* alone; the *I* is *all* there is. *I* am God alone. Not I, John, or John, I, but *I, I!*

There is no "I" as Mary, John, you, me. It is *I*, God; God, *I. I*, Spirit; Spirit, *I. I*, without birth, without creation, age, time or end. I, without matter, mortality, personality, self. *I*, without sin; *I*, without change. *I*, without problem, sickness, sorrow, death. "I am the eternal, the true God; this is my name; I yield my glory to none other" (Isa. 42:8 Moffatt).

Let us now answer the first question, which is, "Can there be one God and many of us?" We know there is one God only, yet we see many of us. As an illustration which will throw some light on this subject, let us consider a tree and its leaves. In your mind, you can see one tree with many leaves. Of course, you must know at the outset that this tree in your mind is an idea, which is immaterial and incorporeal. Now consider carefully a question which I will ask you: What is the relation of a leaf of this tree to the tree? Generally, one's first answer is that the leaf is part of the tree, or the leaf is one with the tree. These answers will not do, for the reason that *ideas in mind cannot be separated into parts.* Inasmuch as the tree *includes* leaves, the answer may very well be this: *the leaf is the tree.*

However, we can expand our vision even beyond this answer, as you will presently see. You may have believed that the greater cannot be put into the lesser. Certainly this statement is not made from the basis of spiritual or cosmic Consciousness which basis alone is Truth; for here there is no size, weight, space or measurement— no greater or lesser. No space exists in our mind, nor can an idea in mind be measured. We can entertain the idea "forest" as easily as we can a single tree. Mind, or Spirit, knows Its world to be spiritual ideas and forms. No outer world of structural or material objects exists. Remember this! Spirit is All; thus, all is Spirit. Turn your attention again to the tree illustration, and this time expand your vision to behold that in Mind, there is no greater or lesser thing. Everything is immeasurable and inseparable. Since the tree is not in parts, but is a whole, then the whole of the tree is "tree" throughout. The full perception of this arresting fact should now be your inspiration that—*the tree is the leaf.*

Cosmic Consciousness is the dominant note of today! In this Consciousness we perceive that Life, Mind, Being is a whole, without parts; that the one Being is the same Being everywhere, throughout Its infinitude. As our love for Reality deepens, and fuller revelation is revealed to us, our vision and our understanding are identical. Previously, revelation disclosed to us the astonishing fact that I-Mary, I-John, am the one Mind, the one Being, Spirit, God. Now, in the light of the new revelation—that God is a whole, and therefore God must be seen and known as a whole everywhere and throughout—the glorious illumination must be that it is God, the one Mind and Being, which is I-Mary, I-John; you, me, us.

The fullness and allness of God is in you, in me, and in everyone, for the fullness and allness of God is everywhere the same One. We are the One by virtue of the fact that the One *is* us. This insight and awareness completely dissipates the belief of many selves, many minds, many individuals and many of us. God—as a whole—is infinite individuality. Distinctiveness and variation of beauty, color, outline and form are in and of the One-All, which is here, is there, is everywhere the same One. It is you, It is me, It is everyone, without sin, without change—pure, perfect, complete.

The Practice of Reality

Ontology includes not only the true facts of Being but also their practice. Health, harmony, happiness and the abundance of all good are answers which can be reached as we, the Self, think and act from our God-state, or standpoint of perfection, as our All-in-All. "By their fruits ye shall know them," is the Christ-edict for all time. Our daily experience of health, harmony and the abundance of good determines for us the exact extent of our spiritual knowledge and exercise thereof, even as our success in mathematics is measured only by our ability to obtain correct answers to its problems.

Presuming that the reader of this work has studied the author's textbook of ontology called *The Great Answer*, let us now summarize the Trinity of Being thus: *I*, the Self, am All. *I* include the perfect principles or facts of being. *I* include perfect awareness and perfect activity. *I* include perfect body and perfect universe. Besides Me there is none else.

We should understand right now that we are Totality; that nothing exists outside of us. There is nothing, therefore, which can or does oppose us. I am Self-Being-Spirit. I am one Infinitude, one Totality, one All-in-All. From this basis, we can see clearly that nothing is to be considered as originating elsewhere than in us.

Each one is *I*, since the *I* is infinitely identified. In every one of us there is the same God-state (Father); the same right and might to think and act from the viewpoint of perfection as ever present and at hand (Son); the same light and illumination to be revealed (Holy Ghost).

Illumination has revealed that we should not continue to place "God" as synonymous with "Self," or "I," but rather understand this word to denote the same meaning as "Father," or our state of perfection. God, the Father, is the first "person" of the Trinity. This God-Father represents perfection, our perfect state of being, body and universe. God is the very Truth; the principle of Being which is immovable, incorruptible, absolute; that to which nothing can be added nor anything taken away. This God-perfection is ever included in the *I*, or us.

Will the reader please draw a circle on a separate paper, to be used for a definite and practical illustration. In the circle draw two horizontal lines so as to divide it into three equal parts. In the first space you may write the following:

I am the Self. *I* am the Father, God, Perfection. *I* am the Absolute, Reality, Truth.

I am Spirit, Being, Life, Love, Mind, Creator, Body, Universe. *I* am the One, Totality, All.

The second position of the Trinity is called the Son. This position of our Self is our activity; our consciousness or awareness; our free will. This is where we think, feel, see, hear, taste, smell, live and act. Presumably, we have all discovered that our mind can think good thoughts or otherwise; we can make good or create evil. Here, then, is the place of light and darkness; waking and sleeping; in fact, free will. Therefore in the middle space you may write the following:

I am the Son. *I* am consciousness, awareness, activity, thinking; feeling, hearing, seeing, tasting, smelling; living, loving, creating. *I* am free will.

When we think and live from the standpoint of the God-state, that is, when we incorporate the facts of reality in our thinking and living, then our experience is one of happiness, harmony and wholeness. When the Father and Son, Perfection and consciousness, become one, this then culminates in the Holy Ghost, or spiritual illumination, which is the third position of the Trinity.

In the third space, you may therefore write the following:

I am the Holy Ghost. *I* am insight, revelation, illumination. *I* am the experience of my Self. *I* am the Christ. *I* am heaven.

It is we who have free will, not God! We, the "I," ever have the will to remain in the "Father's house," (think from the basis of Perfection) or not, as we choose. It is obvious that we are all doing this every day, is it not? When we are not dwelling in the God-state, but turn from it, it may then be said that we represent the "prodigal," that we "sleep and dream," that we function as "man." You see, such choice as this could never be part of God: for "Thou (God) art of purer eyes than to behold evil, and canst not look on iniquity" (Hab.1:13).

Therefore, properly speaking, the "I" and "God" are not synonymous terms. We are the "I," and all the while we are free to choose. We find that we think rightly some of the time, but not always. God, however, is always good, always perfection, always fulfillment, without beginning or end. Thus, God is our perfect state of being.

When we function in the God-state, or state of perfection, then we are in our proper position, and in this state we see all things as they really are. This state always abides within us! We include, and are, all. We are the circle; we are the totality; we are the Triune One. When we admit only reality, only perfection, as our All-in-All, when we continuously dwell in the God-state, then our consciousness is the Christ-consciousness and is our Savior. Thus the Christ is still our redeemer and our deliverer from all darkness and sleep.

Perfect body, perfect universe, are ever prepared, finished and at hand. However, until we think, act and live from the standpoint of the truth, the perfect facts and principles of Being, we cannot consciously experience them nor enter into the perfect answer, which is heaven. Perfect happiness and satisfaction can never be found in any other way. Thus, a partial acceptance of our perfect God-state, a partial awareness of our perfect body and universe as ever present and at hand, delivers to us a degree of harmony, happiness, wholeness and abundance. Ever our consciousness must expand and enlarge in order that we rise from glory to glory, and so finally come unto the measure of the stature of the fullness of Christ, even as did our beloved Jesus.

THE PERFECT WORLD

The general idea of the world before us is that it is external to us; thus it has been termed the world "without." Inasmuch as here appears discords, disasters, wars and limitations of every kind, in our great and sincere desire to practice seeing only the good and the true, there was instituted the method of turning from this world to a world claimed to be "within," and here was pictured a perfect and ever harmonious universe, with no evil whatsoever.

To repeat, desiring not to witness discordant appearances, there began the practice to turn away from the world altogether and to create another world free from all discords and limitations. Although such practice may have helped and benefited many, now that a new light has dawned, we are to soar beyond it: for such a mental procedure assumes that the world we see and call "out there" is not the real and true one. Is this not so?

Now then, when you sleep and in your dream see a world of people, landscape, animals and so forth, these are, of course, all within you; still, you see them as though they were "out there," do you not? In like manner, the very people, animals, land, water, etcetera, which you behold in your waking state, and have called the "without," are not external at all, for the simple reason that inasmuch as you are conscious of them, they exist in and of you. In fact, nothing that we see is ever external to us, for we are the infinite All.

If one turns to an imaginative mental world as the real and the true, what then about this world in which we eat and drink; this world wherein we work and play, act and sleep; this world wherein we see so much of beauty, grandeur and loveliness about us? In thinking most earnestly about this subject lately, suddenly with light and glory it was revealed to me that the world which has been termed the "without," is actually the real world "within us." I saw that any other mental world, so-called "within," is but imaginative: for since it is consciousness which sees, hears and enjoys this world, then this very world before us is the very world within us! The true world is ever with us, the Self. To the extent that we know the truth about our Self, do we come to know the truth about our world also.

Lo, this world wherein we walk, live, move and breathe is the actual world, the kingdom-of-heaven world—in fact, the only universe there is. Believing this world to be a picturing forth of all sorts of lack, discord and limitation, the tendency has been to turn away from it, even as Moses fled from the rod when to him it appeared as a serpent. Moses learned, however, that his own Being could teach him all things; that his own Being is all-knowing and Self-revealing: and so shall we all learn the same.

The Rod and the Serpent

In Exodus, fourth chapter, we find the revelation of the rod and the serpent. When Moses came back to the rod from which he had fled, lo, he saw there no serpent at all, but the rod only: he saw it had been a rod all the time. Similarly, never has anything but good been in our universe. Verily, this world, dear friends, the place whereon we now stand, is the city beautiful, the promised land, the heavenly world, regardless of how we view it.

When Moses fled from what he believed a serpent, he was actually turning from the rod, that is, from reality. He needed not to destroy a serpent, nor unsee it nor treat it nor handle it. He needed but to bring himself face to face with the thing which appeared as a serpent and right here, in this place, see the rod. This new point of view you will find to be the simple and pure reality.

There is but one world, and you, the Self, are seeing it, walking in it, enjoying it. This world of the Self is filled with beauty, charm, harmony, peace, loveliness and all similar quantities. It is without spot or blemish; without war, discord or limitation of any kind. It is the universe of Spirit; it is the heavenly land; it is paradise.

How then shall one regard such appearances called war, discords, lack and limitations? The same as when one reports a serpent in a rod. First of all, let us recognize that the "serpent" (war) needs no direct treatment of any kind. Had Moses wanted to get rid of the serpent which he believed he was seeing, how foolish an idea to destroy it, pray over it, deny it or cope with it in any other way. But how quickly and easily it vanished from view when he saw with the correct viewpoint!

Thus we include mind; but mind is not a proper synonym for God.

The war of today is the result of imperfect and improper viewpoint of reality. It will vanish when the pure principle of Being is more generally accepted and practiced. All the while Moses thought he saw a serpent, he was actually seeing the rod, for it was this he was looking at. How foolish had he prayed to God to take away the serpent! Just as futile today to ask God to end the war. God includes nothing but perfection; the same as in good there is no evil whatsoever; and in mathematics there is no mistake.

Any one of us may believe or say that two plus two are five, but none of us can ever actually see it. From this simple illustration we can understand that incorrect answers to life and being may be mentally experienced, but never actually seen. Such experience is like any dream. There are no events in a dream; no reality to it. All the time the Self, His world, and His true experience continue on, uninterrupted. The practice of the Self, therefore, is Its practice of reality. The Self practices being the perfect Self, being intelligent, perfect Mind; practices living in the perfect world where there is no evil anywhere. In no other way can we practice the living Truth, which we are, and function as the Christ-consciousness.

If one desires to know perfection, he must see perfection and believe in perfection as his

All-in-All; he must see that his "earth is full of the goodness of the Lord" (Ps. 33:5). Of course, the Self is the Lord. How could the wolf and the lamb, for instance, dwell together, and the leopard lie down with the kid and the desert rejoice and blossom as the rose, unless this were the way they really are today and ever? Perfection of being is not a matter of evolution, but remains the same state "yesterday, today, and forever." "That which hath been is now; and that which is to be, hath already been" (Eccles. 3:15).

When we see from the standpoint of reality or principle that we are actually living now in the kingdom, never having left it, and are ever experiencing our perfect state, regardless of any dream, then our report shall be, "Violence shall no more be heard in thy land, wasting nor destruction within the borders ... Thy people shall be righteous" (Isa. 60:18-21). Indeed, the "new heaven and new earth," which we are destined to see and experience as it really is, is not another dwelling place, but the same world seen in the correct way.

There is no such thing as two worlds, one without and one within us; one unreal and temporal, the other real and eternal. These are but two ways of looking at the same thing. To actually understand and accept this world before us as the genuine, the real and the true, brings one into a new sense of things altogether. Remember, the serpent was no part of the rod, and no more are wars, tribulations and vicissitudes part of our kingdom of heaven. As the real and the true are more fully accepted by us and more perfectly practiced, vain imaginations vanish. Thus to practice the reality of Being, we, the Self, understand and act upon the eternal truth that this world before us is our real and true universe! This world before us, whereon our feet tread, is the very world within us! There is no other!

"I go to prepare a place for you," said the incomparable Jesus. He paved the way; he illustrated the steps which we must take in order now and here to consciously see and experience the world which is indeed the universe of the Self. So our world before us will again appear free from war when we exercise our right and might to increase our consciousness of oneness and indivisibility. Then will spring forth a new and universal order of living for all people. This new order will usher in universal peace, harmony and prosperity, virtually the kingdom of heaven on earth, which for nearly two thousand years the whole world has been praying.

As Moses was led to see the nothingness of illusion and the presence of the real only, so likewise as we function in the Christ-consciousness shall we all be brought into the knowledge and awareness that the perfect is really all there ever is before us.

HEAVEN

Heaven, comprising perfection, wholeness, peace, harmony, beauty and plenty, forever exists for one and for all alike, but must be discovered and accepted before one comes into an experience thereof. It is by no means merely a location where unlimited good abounds, yet such a heavenly place may be found right here, or wherever we are. All experience is heaven to us to the extent that we exercise our spiritual vision, might and right to behold the perfection of being—perfect self, perfect body, perfect universe—as ever present and at hand.

The trite metaphysical saying that, "Heaven is a state of consciousness," may infer that there is no perfect world, body or Self beyond one's awareness at the time. Such an assumption is altogether incorrect. Regardless of what our state of consciousness is, all the while the perfect and true world stands before our vision; we manifest the spiritual, perfect body; we are the one and only Self and Being. We, the Self, the divine Us, the I AM THAT I AM, fill all space and are Totality: there is none else.

Now then, the way one looks at a thing, sees, hears and is conscious of it, may not at all accord with what is actual, real and present in his midst. Thus so long as he persists in the abstract statement that, "All is consciousness," he may be overlooking the supreme fact that God, the perfect state of being, including the perfect expression, body and universe, already exists in manifested form.

For instance, the real world before us is the real world within us; nor is it as perfect as one sees it, for regardless how he views it, it remains the finished kingdom, at hand. It is free from evil; it is the land of peace, joy, harmony, beauty and delight. "... and the generations of the world are healthful: and there is no poison of destruction in them, nor the kingdom of death upon the earth" (Wisd. of Sol. 1:14 Apocrypha).

Jesus declared, "The kingdom of God is within you!" Here the Greek word for "within" is *entos*, meaning "in the midst." For the Lord himself, being asked by some when his kingdom should come, said, "When the two shall be one, and the outside as the inside" (New Sayings of Jesus).

Verily, the kingdom of God is our own Self and Being; and this kingdom of good comes in our midst to the degree that we recognize and accept it as the only real and true experience there is; the everlasting and unchangeable reality of Being.

We, Self, possess all knowledge, nevertheless must experience this knowledge through our daily living: and this we do through our active awareness or consciousness of it. We might possess a fine automobile, for instance, but what value would it be to us unless it were put into use or into motion? Therefore, our correct use or practice of mind determines our daily experience of health, harmony, and abundance.

Neither our mind nor body depends upon our state of consciousness! Our state of consciousness, however, determines the extent of the enjoyment of our perfect Self and body. We use mind for thinking, the same as we use eyes for seeing. We are ever in a state of Self-knowing, termed consciousness, and this constitutes our daily experience.

To repeat: We are unconditioned Self and body; perfect, absolute, complete. Our mind may report understanding or belief. Understanding is based on and represents Principle, Reality. Belief has no foundation whatsoever and is illusion. The nature of Being, or Self, is to enjoy and experience Its wonder, power and glory; and this comes to pass according to the conscious awareness of Itself as all there is. Such consciousness comprises Its thinking, feeling, seeing, hearing and acting.

Then the saying, "Heaven is a state of consciousness," rightly understood, means that our present experience of ˙health, harmony, peace, success and blessedness is contingent upon our consciousness, on our present awareness of peace, harmony, wholeness, perfection, love, success, abundance, power and glory as ever our very own, here and in our midst, to be utilized on the instant.

We will never know all of our Self at any one time, since this would produce a state of limitation, whereas we are limitless because of our infinitude. The Self does not progress or expand; neither does Its embodiment or expression. Consciousness does, however. In fact, consciousness is continually expanding, as it rises from a boundless basis, and so our daily experience should be one of constant and uninterrupted progress and advancement in every direction. Said the Christ, "I am come that they might have life (be aware that they are life), and that they might have it more abundantly (enjoy it in an ever-increasing manner)."

The Self abides in heaven; the Self is heaven. Harmony, love, happiness is indeed the nature of the Self, and for us to experience this nature is for us to experience heaven. Real happiness, of course, is spiritual, that is, it is in and of such things as belong to reality and eternity; never to illusion or dream. For happiness to be real and to endure, it must necessarily be founded upon purity, love and holiness. Moreover, we should know that never is it dependent upon certain people, times or circumstances but is the Self's awareness of Its own wonder, glory and power. Thus our happiness cannot really be interrupted nor restricted in any way.

So long as we are conscious of discord or limitation and accept it as real or true, we are not functioning our mind from the standpoint of reality, but of the dream. In order to see and feel our perfection as it really is, we must operate as the Christ-consciousness, the Mind that is without dream. True or Christ-consciousness can know no limitation or distress of any kind; ever it can have perfect confidence in its work, for knowing the principle or reality involved, it knows the result is assured. Therefore, through our Christ-consciousness we come into our perfect experience called heaven.

THE PERFECT BODY

The same spiritual viewpoint applies to the body as to the world. Our body is our expression, even as is our world. It is not an effect, but is Our-self, since we and our embodiment are the same one.

There is but one I-Life-Being, but one manifestation-expression-body. This, together with consciousness, comprises the totality or infinitude of Being. The one I-Life-Being is not divided nor subdivided into separate parts, particles or individualities but is infinitely indivisibilized; and its infinite indivisibility is its infinite individuality, ever operating as the whole. Thus the body is one, yet infinite in expression: always the one Substance, the one Life, the one Being.

Ever the body is as perfect as the *I* am and as immortal, eternal and incorruptible. Any appearance of discord in the body is the result of improper viewpoint; and so, in his daily living, one experiences in accordance with his conscious awareness of that which is eternal and true. One need therefore never treat nor handle the so-called sickness or limitation in any way, any more than he would attempt to alter the serpent appearing in the rod. Nor need anything be done to bring out health or harmony in the body, since always and ever it is present and never could be changed nor affected in any way.

The act of truth which constitutes the treatment is our awareness of the Self-body as It everlastingly is—perfect and immaculate always. My declarations and enforcement must be from this basis and none other! Really, no pain can or does exist in Being, and so no one is actually experiencing it; a dream is always nothing. There are no laws governing or controlling us but those we admit and sanction; therefore we should accept only the law of perfection: changeless and eternal.

Furthermore, we are to know and enforce the fact that there is no other false mind seeing, thinking, or feeling any discord, as might seem to be the case; that we, the Self, have power almighty and are equal to any emergency, since our ability to know harmony and immutability as ever intact and at hand is ever-present, indivisible and absolute. I need to keep my mind stayed on my reality, my unalterable harmony.

If I am conscious of some disharmony or discord, or accept it in thought (mind), then I am living and thinking in a dream. Therefore in order to waken, I must begin at once to think and act from the basis and standpoint of my reality. I must identify myself as the Christ-consciousness, the mind which remains awake and is not dreaming. Thinking as the Christ-mind, I soon find my peace, wholeness and harmony to be present and intact.

While we dwell in the God-state no harm can ever befall us. Our consciousness of this almighty truth, our awareness that we are the infinite One, constitutes our almighty power of deliverance; and "the gates of hell shall not prevail against it" (Matt. 16:18). I, as the Christ-consciousness, can maintain and preserve my health, harmony and prosperity by thinking from the viewpoint of reality. I know my body to be Spirit, or spiritual, never having been otherwise. Ever my prerogative is to uphold my life and being as omnipotent, omniscient and omnipresent, even as did our illustrious Jesus. This is the reason for my existence; this my destiny and eternality.

The Self and the body exist as one whole. Never should they be thought of as two, but always only as a unit. I, the Self, do not depend upon the body, nor the body upon the Self. These two are one perfection, without shadow of turning; never to be evolved or developed, but ever and always existing as the perfect manifested whole.

My body is perfect now; your body is perfect now; always Spirit, or spiritual. When we say that body is one, we mean that all body is the one Substance, the one Life, Self, Being. The one Self is infinitely identified as you, as me, and as all who are life: so likewise is the one body.

Now then, these facts about ourself and body are not only to be known as Self-existent, but we are to enforce them, so as to experience their fulfillment in our daily living. It is not enough, for instance, that mathematics exists in a perfect state, but we need to exercise or practice it in our mathematical problems in order to experience its ever-existent correct answers. Only our consciousness, or active knowing and enforcing of the facts of being, enables us to enter into the certain experience thereof. *I Am!* I must *know* that *I Am!* I must *enforce* what *I Am!*

Jesus knew his body to be Spirit, or spiritual; and moreover, he also knew this to be true for others. Gloriously he proved to all and for all time, that neither crucifixion nor the grave could take life from the body! The power dwelt in him, both to lay down his life and to take it up again. Never did he believe his body to be at the mercy of circumstances. Verily the crucifixion and resurrection set forth the undeniable and irrefutable fact that the body is one with Life Itself, therefore, ever immutable and incorruptible. Jesus' ascension climaxed his illustrious career, for he left no body among us. It vanished with him when he withdrew himself from us.

Thinking of some imaginative other body to exist within us, perfect and spiritual, instead of the very body which we are expressing at the moment, restricts our present demonstration of health and harmony as here and now. As this world before us is the perfect universe, and nothing less, so also this body with which we walk, live and have expression is the perfect body, and nothing else. When this fact becomes more fully comprehended and enforced, the seeming limits of time, conditions, thoughts and beliefs will then have vanished.

The belief that there is a hidden other body somewhere to be brought forth, and that the body now visible and before us is not the real and true one, prolongs one's bondage and limitation today. As there is only one universe, and we are now living in it, so also there is but one body, and we are now expressing it. The correction therefore must be in our viewpoint and never toward universe or body.

The notion that we are each an individual life and being, with an individual body, seems difficult for many to relinquish. First, it must be seen that we are not one of many, for *I* am one Life, Being, the whole, which is indivisible. The body, for instance, is composed of many different organs, nevertheless, the body is one. So life or being is composed of many different people, shall we say, nevertheless life or being is one. When the word *individual* is used, one is apt to think of some one or thing separate from the whole. None of us can be separated from the whole. We are all the selfsame substance, life and being; the selfsame *I* which is one totality.

As, for instance, the blood courses through each finger of our hand, yet is the same blood; and all the cells and skin of the fingers belong not to the fingers themselves, but rather to the body as a whole; so the life which we are living, the principle of truth which we are practicing, belongs not to us as so many separate people or individuals, but to us all as one whole.

True, there are no two leaves of a tree exactly alike; yet all leaves go to make up the tree, nor could a single leaf exist apart therefrom. Naturally, we are as the leaves, that is, no two of us are exactly alike, for the *I* of Self is infinitely diversified (or individualized, if you prefer to use this word). You can see, however, that much of the so-called differences are but part of the dream.

Certainly it is true that we have distinctive talents and that we make use of our intelligence in various and multitudinous ways. Paul expressed this idea very clearly in his epistle to the Corinthians. The entire chapter is very illuminating: "There are diversities of gifts, but the same Spirit ... But all these worketh that one and the selfsame Spirit ... " (1 Cor. 12:4, 11).

I, The Self, The Only Creator

In Isaiah, 45th chapter, 7th verse, we read the following startling and arresting declaration: "I form the light, and create darkness; I make peace and create evil. I the Lord do all these things." A surface reading of this verse gives rise to the belief that God not only is responsible for all the evils in the world today, but actually creates them. Such a belief at once assumes evil to be as real as good.

Now then, what is the meaning of the word *real*? It means to be actual or true. The meaning of the word *true* or *truth* is to be constant, unchangeable, eternal. Therefore anything, to be real, must incorporate the qualities of genuineness, constancy, unchangeableness and eternality. Reasoning upon such intelligence as this, can it be stated correctly that war, for instance, is real and true? Of course not! War began and war will end. The belief that it is real and actual but aids in perpetuating its appearance.

The Bible would group all evils under the word *sin*. According to the Bible as a whole, it is sin which is the root cause of all evil. It was metaphysics that broadened this outlook and introduced the idea that sickness, too, should be put in the same category as sin; also poverty and limitation of every kind. The next point of view must be to understand the meaning of the word *evil*. Even the great majority who consider sin, sickness, poverty, war and death as unrealities, nevertheless look upon them as evils. For instance, is it not a fact that you regard the war as evil? Do you not think of sickness, sin, poverty or limitation as evil? In fact, are you not regarding all forms of discord or limitation as evils which can be removed by Truth? Right here is where a deeper and more illumined perception or awareness needs to take place. A quickening of the Spirit is required which will permit a larger and fuller view of the baffling assertion, "I make peace, and create evil. I the Lord do all these things."

Just how can one truthfully declare, "God is all," and at the same time regard sickness, sin, war or poverty as evil? Do you see what I mean? If, in your treatment, you assert that God, good, is all, how then can you also assert that war, for instance, is evil? Or how could you assert that it is real? On the other hand, how could you accept that, "I, the Lord, make peace, and create evil"?

Today we, the Self, seem to hear about a war, do we not? We, the Self, (there is no other) seem to see sickness, disease, sin and various forms of discords and limitations about us. Is this not so? Jesus came into this world for a great purpose. What was that purpose? To rid the world of evil or evil appearances? No, for there seems as much now as then. To destroy anything whatsoever? Let Jesus, the Christ, answer in his own words: "I am not come to destroy, but to fulfill" (Matt. 5:17). "For judgment I am come into this world, that they which see not might see; and that they which see might be made blind" (John 9:39). "I am come that they might have life, and that they might have it more abundantly" (John 10:10). "I am come a light into the world, that whosoever believeth on me should not abide in darkness" (John 12:46).

Jesus caused all kinds of sickness and disease to vanish, thereby proving they were neither real nor true. He spoke of some of these people as being possessed with a devil; other times he said they "sleep." Still on other occasions, he set forth his understanding in a very clear and definite fashion. For instance, when Lazarus was considered by his sisters and others to be sick unto death, they sent word to Jesus, saying, "Lord, behold, he whom thou lovest is sick." Jesus' reply was, "This sickness is not unto death, but for the glory of God." Nevertheless, "He abode two days still in the same place where he was."

At the grave of Lazarus, we find Jesus saying to Martha, "Said I not unto thee, that if thou wouldest believe, thou shouldest see the glory of God?" (John 11:40). Here he plainly alluded to sickness, and even death, as a place where the Self might be glorified. In fact, later on, in alluding to himself, he signified "by what death he should glorify God" (John 21:19).

At another time Jesus was questioned by his disciples regarding a certain man who was blind from birth. They said, "Master who did sin, this man, or his parents, that he was born blind?" Here they wanted to discover the basic cause for this evil. However, Jesus replied, "Neither hath this man sinned nor his parents." In plain words, neither of them had committed any evil, therefore, none was present. He then continued, "but that the works of God should be made manifest in him." There was only one reason in this case for the blindness—that here could take place the practice of reality!

The self could here practice being God, being omnipotent and indivisible. Verily, our God-perfection, wholeness, immortality, indivisibility, must be practiced. For in what other way can the self realize it is All?

I am come to show you how to practice being perfection. I am come that they which have not seen this reality, might now see it, and that they which see sickness or trouble of any kind might become blind to it. I am come a light, an example, a revelation into the world, that whosoever practices reality should not continue in sleep (darkness), but waken to reality.

Perhaps all of us, at times, have thought of sickness, discord or limitation of any kind as annoying problems or troubles; in fact as evils. But there is a much better and truer way to regard them. It was this very viewpoint that Isaiah was trying to convey to his people; that is, that we are the *only* Creator; that *I*, the Lord-Self, am all.

Really, that which anyone may be considering an evil in his life is but a place where he may waken to the glorious reality that perfection is really all there is. Never are there two opposing powers, good and evil. *I*, the Self, make good and create evil. *I*, the Self, am All.

In attempting to overcome war with war, for instance, of course the darkness remains darkness. But think how the Self might be exalted if only here, in this place, a new and higher order of living were seen and established! Progress, advancement, expansion inevitably must come to pass, since ever the Self must become *increasingly* aware of Allness. Experience is the Self's fulfillment of Itself.

Today there needs to take place a simpler and more universally higher type of government. It cannot be prohibited; in spite of any nation or nations, it is coming to pass. Wars need not take place, but if universal consent to universal progress, expansion, betterment is not forthcoming, then war is the result. In this new light, can you see that there is no evil power causing the war and that though war seems such a monstrous evil, still it need not be, if nations will but consent to national progress, expansion and advancement toward a new and higher order of living in all directions?

There must come a new dispensation for all, which will usher in a new and greater wealth, happiness, prosperity and peace than ever before dreamed of. The Self must know Itself; constantly and increasingly enjoy and experience Its majesty, power, wonder and glory!

Problems force the Self to function more and more from the basis of perfection, that is, from the true facts and principles of Being. How could reality be practiced if there were no occasion, no necessity for the Self to ever increasingly know and express Itself? Such a necessity is by no means evil, as is generally thought. Really, in the true sense, there is no evil; but rather a place where the Self shall be glorified: that the works of God should be made manifest, in you, in me, in this nation, in that nation, over all the world, everywhere.

Do you consider mathematical problems as evil? Of course not. Moreover, of what use would mathematics be without mathematical problems? Similarly, how could Being enlarge Its awareness of Its perfection and completeness, Its infinite good and harmony, if there arose no opportunities for expansion? No one regards mathematical problems as evil, but rather as essentials to knowledge.

The Self is Omniscience! The Self should ever be expanding and *advancing* in the conscious awareness of Its allness, Its infinity, Its almighty power and glory. Naught can stop, stay, or hinder It, since naught but the Self exists. Said *I* not unto thee, that if thou wouldest believe in the oneness and allness of the Self, thou shouldest see the glory of God, the Self, expressed as life more abundantly, everywhere?

Problems force us to expand our consciousness, and so participate in fuller and greater light. We should therefore cease thinking of problems as evils, and instead, know that since we created them, we can also dissolve them and cause them to utterly vanish. The very fact that we (and not some other power) create them is what gives us power to demolish them. Therefore cease to *contend* with some other force or power; use your intelligence as power in the right direction. Nothing exists outside of you!

We may remain awake and aware of good, or may partake of sleep and dream of its absence. In this case, all that is needed is our awakening; an opening of our insight and perception to the fact that we have almighty power to let go the dream and again function from our real and true estate of perfection, ever-existent, here, and at hand. When we sleep and dream, are we not still in our own rooms, safe and secure? No matter where we are dreaming we are, we are really only in our own rooms; our body is there, our life is there, our entire self and being is there. In the same way, regardless of our dream of sickness, lack, war or limitation of any kind, we are living in the perfect universe; we are expressing the perfect body, and our God-perfection has never been separated from us.

You may ask: How can it be true that I can think good and evil; I can do right and wrong; I can remain awake and go to sleep, yet still declare, "I am the Truth; I am God; I and my Father are one"? Again you may ask: I read that God is unchangeable, invariable, absolute, without shadow of turning; therefore, how can I reconcile myself with God? In only one way: by seeing that God means your perfect state of being! The word *God* means good, perfection, reality. Therefore, as light can never be darkness, so also perfection is never imperfection. God is invariable and immovable. God includes the perfection of the self, body and universe. Reality never changes! It is without beginning or end. God is our reality, unalterable and intact.

This fact I must prove for myself. I must find out all this for myself. This is the joy of my existence. As the answers to all mathematical problems are included in its principles, to be reached through intelligence and insight, so our answers, our fulfillments called happiness, health, harmony, peace and prosperity are all included in God, our perfection, our principle and reality, to be discovered and experienced as we seek and find, knock and have it opened; speak and have our word come to pass.

How much of mathematics would one know without participating in the solution of its problems? Little or none. How much of God, or Perfection, can we know and experience without bringing our hearts and thoughts into the awareness and recognition thereof? Little or none. While we sleep, we deprive ourselves of the awareness and activity of our waking states, do we not? Yet in our sleeping dreams, we may waken ourselves to our normal state. Likewise, now and here, while we seem to be confronted with problems called lack or limitation of any kind, we may indeed waken to our reality, our perfect Self, body and universe, untouched by any dream; beautiful, luminous, irresistible. But we must so choose! We must so desire! We must so insist upon doing!

Jesus did it. He said that we can do it. Inevitably, we must. This time is now at hand; not only for people singly, but for nations and for the entire world. You will find the third chapter of Joel very illuminating: "Wake up the mighty men ... Let the weak say, I am strong ... Let the heathen be wakened ... Multitudes, multitudes in the valley of decision: for the day of the Lord is near in the valley of decision ... so shall ye know that I am the Lord your God dwelling in Zion."

Those who come into peace and prosperity shall be those who decide to turn to God, our perfect finished estate of good, in every direction. Why call upon God, our perfect state, to do that which is already done and finished? The principle of mathematics does not need to solve its problems.

We, the Self, we alone must awaken, choose, decide, arise, come forth, return and remain in our perfect state of consciousness which is the Christ!

Here we see aright; we see perfection, God, as indeed All-in-All. We see that really we live, move, and have our being in God, Perfection, and never have we actually been severed from It. But as in a dream of sleep we may be dissatisfied, fearful and distressed, and our only actual escape from the dream would be to awaken from the sleep, so also, our only genuine release from the dreams of war, discord and limitation is to awaken in consciousness to our God-state, our perfect Self, body and universe as *right here where we are*, intact and ever present.

Perfection is all. *I*, God, or the perfect state, am the All and the Only, without beginning or end. Beside Me, the perfect, there is none else. *I*, Perfection, fill all space. To light there is no darkness. To perfection there is no imperfection. To reality there is no unreality. "What concord has Christ with Belial?" (2 Cor. 6:15). How then can we reconcile light and darkness? The waking and sleeping states? We cannot!

All the time we sleep and dream, everything there is of us is in our waking state: our life, our intelligence, our body, our world. Now then, in order for us to leave the dream, we should think of our waking state; this in itself will force an awakening. Therefore, if you are in a mental sleep, dreaming discord of any kind, turn yourself to your waking state, which is your perfect state, and think of it as your genuine reality; and here you must dwell.

However, in order that we become aware or conscious of these existing facts, we must give up ignorance, false beliefs and their spectralities and function consciously from the state of Intelligence and Reality. Do not place a scandal upon your mind because it may think imperfectly, any more than upon your eyes because they report the meeting of sky and trees. You would not place any blame upon your eyes in such an instance, and no more should mind be considered imperfect because of false thinking. We, the Self, are the one who sees, hears, thinks. Imperfect thinking must therefore be traced to us. We are above mind and above body. As we think from the standpoint of our perfection and reality, we become aware of it, and so fulfill our Self and Being.

Always remember this: our perfection is God, really the one and only state of Being. We become aware of this God-perfection to the extent that we believe in it, accept it, worship and adore it, lay down all thoughts and things for it, and come to claim and take possession of it as our very own.

Let us hasten to function in God, our perfect state! We find David demanding of himself: "Awake, why sleepest thou, O Lord? arise cast us not off forever" (Ps. 44:23). David is here speaking to himself; he is the "I" which needs to waken; he is the Lord, the one who can choose. David is not addressing God, the perfect state of his being, but arousing himself to function in and from that very state. Thus we are to return to God; return to Perfection in our every thought, act and experience. When we do this, then indeed we have returned to Zion, our real and true existence.

Here there is no sleep, no darkness, no dream. Here our consciousness is the Christ; and we are satisfied to dwell in this, our perfect state, forever.

OUR AGELESS BEING

I am the Self with almighty power. There is none besides Me, none to contradict or oppose Me. How old is the Self? The Self was never born. The Self lives in eternity, never having been separated from it. There is no time in Reality, and no time in a dream. The belief of old age is, in this new light, not an evil in itself; but rather it presents an opportunity for the Self to exercise, at this point, the awareness of Its eternally ageless Being; timeless, limitless, unchangeable.

As the Self, we should think of our flesh as fair as a child's and as firm and smooth. We should maintain beauty, grace and loveliness by becoming more and more aware of them as our own ever present allness, perfection and completeness. Actually, our body is eternally and uninterruptedly perfect in every way. When we entertain an improper viewpoint of it, we are as in a dream, yet here we are afforded an opportunity to know the truth about the dream—that is, that in it no events are transpiring; no one is in a dream; no substance, power, life or action exists in it.

Positively, we are to change our viewpoint from that of dreaming "age" to that of knowing the changeless, ageless loveliness of our eternal Being. The paramount fact to know and enforce is that our body is Spirit, or spiritual, immaculate. Our spiritual body is ever safe and secure, perfect and absolute, unalterable and irresistible. No age ever touched it; no discord or disturbance of any kind ever interfered in any way with its purity, perfection and spirituality. No evil ever needs to be removed from it; no organs or functions set right; nor is any age to be added nor subtracted. Ever our body is beautiful as the morning stars and light as the sun.

CREATING OUR ABUNDANCE

Let us again bring before us the revelation of our Trinity, so that we will better comprehend just how we can supply our world with the things we would like to have expressed here. The first position of the Self is called, "The Father," the second, "The Son," and the third, "The Holy Ghost." We may now set it forth as follows:

1. I am the First and the Last; I am the totality of my world; I include the state of perfect understanding and perfect expression. This state of Being is called God, or Father, meaning principle, reality, the absolute, without shadow of turning. I am the creator of my experience which, in order to be peace, wholeness, happiness and success, must be founded upon perfection, reality, God. Of course, I am Life without beginning or end; I am Intelligence; I am Power; I am the All-in-All.

2. I am ever in a state of activity and awareness of my allness and wholeness. This is called consciousness, the Son. I am continually knowing my infinitude of Being; thus I think, see, hear, feel; and in all my various avenues of awareness come into the knowledge of my Self as all there is. Since I am all, I have free will to be a law unto myself. Functioning from my perfect state, (Father) I enact the Christ.

3. I am the fulfillment of my Self. This fulfillment, answer, or true experience is called the Holy Ghost, since only through my Self-revelation and Self-illumination, I come to express the perfection, power and glory of my being.

My creation is for the glorification of my Self, that the Father, Perfection, may be glorified in the Son, true activity of Being. It is the Principle, Perfection, that I am, which permits and makes possible the works or activities of consciousness (the Son). Ever we should desire that Reality and consciousness, Father and Son, be one; since only in this state does the Perfect become known and experienced. Our God-state, of course, is ever intact and ever in manifestation. To the extent that we become awake to this ever-existent perfection do we fulfill it in our daily living. Thus our knowing and our experiencing go hand in hand.

If we consider the power of thought to be centered in something called Mind, we are depriving ourself of our own sovereignty and power and are unawake to the fact that *I* am the first, and *I* am the last. All there is, including Life, Mind, Spirit, is in and of the *I* which is Alpha and Omega. We think; we live; we act; we feel; we love; and so on. Self-revelation makes all these things clear to us; and this is why we should ever look to our own Self for all light, power and revelation, since looking elsewhere simply deprives one of inspired knowledge and the blessed experience thereof.

Creation is for the purpose of bringing forth the desires of our heart in our daily living. Our experience, of course, depends upon our consciousness, that is, our knowledge of reality and our ability to hold steadfastly to it. Through our illuminated awareness of God, our perfection, we come to express goodness, love, success and happiness. In our present state of awareness, we feel the need for money, home, food, clothing, etc. While such forms as these have no eternal existence, nevertheless we have the right and might to satisfy our desires at every point of our daily experience, even as Jesus multiplied the loaves and fishes.

One must come to see that inasmuch as we are All, we give to ourself and we receive from ourself. This giving and taking constitutes our Self-existence and Self-support. Ever before us should be the immovable platform and axiom: Besides Me, the Self, there is none else. For instance, if you desire employment, who is to give it you? None but yourself. If you have something to sell, who will be your buyer? None but yourself. I am the one who sells and the one who buys. I am the one who gives and the one who takes. Through this activity, I am Self-supporting. If I wish companionship, who is there to supply it? None but I myself. If we deal with Mind, with people, as another, we give to them the power which should rest only in our hands.

Verily this is my dominion and authority: to govern and control my experience from the standpoint that I alone am its creator. Who are those who come to me as my companions, friends or associates? So far as I am concerned, they are my consciousness; but to themselves they are the Self. Until we see that our experience is but our creation or consciousness, we do not think of it as such nor recognize ourself as its creator.

Therefore, until one is fully awake to this realism, he is, more or less, at the mercy of his creation. Thus he may create a Frankenstein which later turns upon him.

It can now be seen that the devil, mortal mind, or error, which in the past has received so much attention, has been nothing at all but one's own creations which, because not known as such, resulted in so much misunderstanding, havoc and tragedy. Whether or not we are aware of it, we are creating all the time; and until we do admit this liberating point and take our position as the maker and creator of it all, we are at its mercy. Thus, no wonder hopes have been thwarted, desires do not come to pass, and experiences fall so short of peace, harmony and prosperity.

One must look to himself! He is his creator of good; he is his own supply of wealth and abundance, prosperity and success. As soon as one is willing to relinquish all other teaching, all other instruction and all other beliefs, and seek only for his own Self and Being to be revealed to him, the illumination and revelation shall not tarry, but shall be found intact and at hand. Ever the Self must discover Itself to be All-sufficient; Self-supplying, Self-sustaining; Self-existent. Thinking from this basis, this absolute principle and reality, we shall know the Self to be the mighty Father, the everlasting Savior. Therefore, "The redeemed (those who look to the Self to include perfection) shall return ... everlasting joy shall be upon their head: they shall attain gladness and joy; and sorrow and mourning shall flee away" (Isa. 51:11).

When we have allowed our Self to be our Savior, our All-in-All, then, "The sun shall be no more thy light by day; neither for brightness shall the moon give light unto thee; but the Lord (your own Self) shall be unto thee an everlasting light, and thy God, (Perfection) thy glory. Thy people (totality) also shall be righteous" (Isa. 60:19,21).

HEALING

What is healing? Is it the changing of conditions? No. Is it the rearrangement of thoughts? No. Is it the adjustment of dreams? No. Healing is one's awakening from sleep and dream.

While it is true that there are no events in a dream nor anyone in a dream, still it is true also that so long as I accept any imperfection before me, I am dreaming. If I see imperfection or hear imperfection or feel imperfection, I can do so only in a dream: I cannot do so in God, my perfect state. If I believe that another is reporting sickness, discord or limitation of any kind, I am forced to admit that insofar as I am concerned, I am dreaming it; for it is certain that all I know of another is my consciousness of him, and were I functioning fully from my God-perfection, I would not be cognizant of imperfection anywhere. Thus it was that after his resurrection Jesus did no healing works of any kind. He was then prepared to "return to the Father," the state of uninterrupted perfection.

Turning to Jesus' life while on earth, we see that, "He is the propitiation for our sins; and not for ours only, but also for the sins of the whole world" (1 John 2:2). Indeed, how else, except as his own consciousness could he have canceled them?

He took upon himself the sins (dreams) of the world, to illustrate to all how we are to prove our reality of Being to be ever present and intact, and how our deliverance from the sleep and dream is to take place. Surely while I sleep, I cannot enter into another's dream! Therefore, all I know of anyone is what I accept of him in my own consciousness. Thus, I should think of all others only as my Self and from the viewpoint of the One. Then I am free to see them according to the standpoint of perfection as my All and Only. I am responsible only for the way I see or view them.

"He was wounded for our transgressions, he was bruised for our iniquities; the chastisement of our peace was upon him; and with his stripes we are healed." So far as his consciousness was concerned, Jesus redeemed us. But so far as our consciousness is concerned, we are to redeem ourself; and not ourself only, but also the sins of the whole world. We are to learn that Perfection, God, is all.

It can be plainly seen that although Jesus healed multitudes of all manner of sickness, for instance, they were sick again, and died. In his world they were perfect, without beginning or end. To him they were his people, the sheep of his pasture, characters in a world of which he was creator. To themselves they had free will to think and to live as they chose; to discover their perfection, at hand.

To myself I am all. I must deal only with my own consciousness. I must not believe in imperfections as existing in my universe. I must continually practice the thinking, feeling and acting that is based upon Perfection, Reality, Principle, my waking (God) state — the only real and true state there is. I must see another only as myself, the Self. I must refuse the imperfection that he presents. I must also refuse to believe that I am powerless to help him: for I have all power over my consciousness. "I am the Lord; that is my name; and my glory will I not give to another" (Isa. 42:8).

Jesus exercised power over all undesirable appearances and spoke to his characters as he chose. Why not, since enacting his realization of Perfection as the All and Only, he possessed supreme power over them? Right here we should recognize the infamy and depravity to rule one's world, and the people in it, from any basis other than that of infinite love and purity; from any ideal other than that of infinite good and harmony. To rule from another viewpoint is to depict imperialism, dominance, tyranny and personal dictatorship.

The 47th chapter of Isaiah clearly and vividly sets forth this erring position and its doom:

> For thou hast trusted in thy wickedness; thou has said, None seeth me. Thy wisdom and thy knowledge, it hath perverted thee; and thou hast said in thine heart, I am, and none else beside me. Therefore evil and mischief and desolation shall come upon thee suddenly.

The same book, 5th chapter, is also most illuminating for today: "Woe unto them that call evil good, and good evil; that putteth darkness for light, bitter for sweet. Woe unto them that are wise in their own eyes, and prudent in their own sight!"

Jesus unequivocally pronounced, "Woe to that man by whom the offense cometh (Matt. 18:7).

To everyone, there is nothing but his own world, his own creation of consciousness. This is exactly what Jesus taught and the basis from which Jesus functioned. He need not have been crucified. He could have stopped it at any moment, had he chosen to do so. However, he elected rather to prove himself superior to the experience called death, to come forth from the tomb whole and complete in every way. No wonder he later declared, "I am the first and the last."

Is it not just that all responsibility for our state of consciousness rests upon us? In what other way could we ever hope to control our world and our creation, except as its Maker and Creator? In this way only do we have power to cast out devils; to speak the Word and have it come to pass; to create a world without war, without sin, and without strife or struggle of any kind; to bring into experience the promised land, the kingdom of heaven; the crystal earth.

The greater our insight and illumination, the more perfect appears our universe of people, things and surroundings. Finally our fulfillment has been brought to pass. This is our ascension.

FULFILLMENT

As the Self, we each write our own Book of Life. Indeed, who else could write our story? To take this enfranchising viewpoint is to simultaneously deliver into our own hands the key which opens for us the door of paradise.

What is the "descent of the Holy Ghost"? It is the opening of our consciousness to admit the light of crystal clear understanding: the comprehension that we alone are the writer of our

Book of Life; that our experience is our own creation. "Tongues of fire" represent the outpouring of understanding from our own luminous awareness. Reaching this Horeb height, we know that what we have made in the first place, we are able to change in the second place. "The Lord (Creator) gave, and the Lord taketh away" (Job 1:21).

As the Lord of our universe, we are therefore to bless our creations in every way, even as did our Exemplar. "Arise, shine: for thy light is come, and the glory of the Lord (true understanding of Being) is risen upon thee" (Isa. 60:1).

To thy world thou shalt "Preach good tidings ... bind up the broken hearted ... give them beauty for ashes ... the garment of praise for the spirit of heaviness ... For as the earth bringeth forth her bud, so the Lord God (the Self, enacting Perfection) will cause righteousness and praise to spring forth before all the nations" (Isa. 61:1,3,11).

As the perfect creators, we are to make the crooked straight and the rough places smooth. We are to lift up our voice with strength. Lift it up, be not afraid. As the perfect creator, we give power to the faint; and to them that have no might we increaseth strength.

We, and our creation, shall mount up with wings as eagles; we shall run, and not be weary; we shall walk, and not faint. Verily, we shall look upon everything in our consciousness (universe) and pronounce it is very good!

We, if we be lifted up from the viewpoint of a creation, to that of the Creator, will draw all characters unto us. "Behold, I create new heavens and a new earth: and the former shall not be remembered, nor come into mind ... and the voice of weeping shall be no more heard ... nor the voice of crying" (Isa. 65:17-19).

Imperishable beauty, harmony, glory are ever mine as the perfect One. Here, I include and express all that is pure, good and enduring. My principle of Being is perfection, and nothing less. Operating this principle, this perfection, I lift the veil of mystery from myself and creation and bring my sovereignty to light.

Perfection is the reality of all things. It is the Alpha and Omega of Being. Ever our Christ-consciousness can prove this to be the fact of existence, everywhere. *I* am perfect love, perfect light, perfect understanding. *I* am the substance of all; the Spirit that quickeneth; the I AM THAT I AM.

Principle and Reality, God and Father, denote our perfect state of Being; our pure intelligence; our immaculate body; our perfect universe: intact, at hand; now and always.

Therefore let us think, live and act from our awareness of Perfection as the All and Only. Verily, we are the God which fills all space ... the divine us ... the totality of Being.

"Let him that is athirst, come. And whosoever will, let him take the water of Life freely" (Rev. 22:17).

Whosoever will, let him begin now, this very day, to write his Book of Life from the standpoint of Perfection as his All and Only. This is *the practice of reality.*

Spiritual Consciousness

"There is a Spirit (spiritual consciousness) in man." Where? Hidden deep in his inner being. As we have external sense, such as eyes and ears, with which to see and hear external, visible things, so have we inner or spiritual sense with which to know and contact spiritual, invisible things.

Spiritual consciousness is this inner vision — where we see God. Spiritual consciousness is this inner hearing — where we listen to the still small Voice. Spiritual consciousness is inner feeling — where we love and understand with the heart.

No matter how great may be one's intellectual knowledge of Truth or how well versed he may be in the letter of the Word, if his heart be untouched, if there is not an irresistible, spiritual love, rising up like a well of living water within the soul, the great purpose of life, for him, has not yet been reached or felt.

To bring the mind only to this instruction is not enough, for the mind tears the words apart to see how they are put together. The mind considers only the outside or letter of the Word. But when one brings his heart, he brings his love and is then ready to have delivered to him the substance—the inspiration and glory of spiritual consciousness.

This mortal must put on immortality. New birth, atonement, is to take place in one, that he may come into a conscious recognition and realization of what God is and what constitutes his eternal life. Spiritual consciousness is this atonement; and atonement is transcension; and transcension is the kingdom of heaven.

At-one-ment is the coalescence or the bringing together of the human mind or sense with our Mind—the divine Mind. It is an act that takes place individually. It means reconciliation, unity, oneness. No longer two, but one. No longer good and bad, life and death in consciousness; but one being having the clear vision of one life, one substance, one power, one reality, only.

When this at-one-ment takes hold of man, he is touched with living flame, his vision so clarified that no longer does he consider opposites, but he now perceives that there is no actual evil, no actual sickness, no actual sin or death. He recognizes that heaven and earth are the same, that is, that which has been termed earth is really heaven seen imperfectly; that evil is not the absence of good, for good is ever present, but what has been called evil is the good seen ignorantly, imperfectly.

As heat absorbs moisture, as air transmutes smoke, so spiritual consciousness transcends human or mortal sense, and this transcension in you—the transcension of the false with the true, the unreal with the real—is at-one-ment or act of spiritual consciousness.

Therefore, one has not to destroy a false external world, a world of sin, sickness, death. Redemption takes place within. One need not go forth to battle with evil as though it were some external force or power, for "the battle is not ours but God's," meaning that spiritual Consciousness is the universal Redeemer.

How shall one possess spiritual consciousness? Shall he reach up as though standing on tiptoe to grasp something over his head or as though to achieve or attain reality? No. Reality, spiritual consciousness, is that which is under his feet, at his elbow, nearer than breathing. We go out externally to purchase external things, such as food, clothing, etc., but we cannot approach an establishment to purchase joy, peace, wealth, health, for these are not external things, to be acquired externally, but they are spiritual inner realities, and one must seek them where they are to be found.

The real Self of every individual is the eternal Truth, changeless, irresistible, triumphant. And the real Self of everyone is all there is to him. Is this not so? Since it is Truth which frees, then we are liberated and find that we possess spiritual consciousness as we realize and act this Truth which we are.

What gave Jesus the power and authority which he exercised? Was it not because he recognized, claimed and acted the Truth of his being? It was this which infuriated the Jews into saying, "For a good work we stone thee not, but for blasphemy; and because thou being a man, makest thyself God."

Since "those who come to Truth must believe that he (Truth) is," then we believe that the divine Mind is our mind, the changeless Life is our life, the divine Christ is our being. We realize and acknowledge in our own hearts that we ourselves are this Truth, this Life, this Love, for there is but one Being, unity, oneness. All false beliefs are then eliminated through spiritual recognition, acknowledgment—an understanding of who and what we are and our acting accordingly.

It has been said that everything in this world is as real as one makes it and no more so. Then one does not have to master materiality, for how can he master a phantom? One masters an illusion in proportion as he perceives and understands its nothingness. Raising the vision, seeing, feeling, understanding the truth of being, one automatically liberates himself from delusion. A false belief has no thinker, for God is the only mind, and there is no substance or power in anything else. Hence, there is no disease in all the world that is not a dream, an illusion, an imagination.

Consider Peter, bound hand and foot within four walls; guards placed before and behind; heavy doors bolted and secured. Looking at the solid walls, the armed, wide-awake soldiers, the heavy chains, he might well ask, how can I escape? But Peter raised his vision and thus transcended the whole situation. Looking away from the world called matter, limited to three dimensions, what did he see? He saw a fourth-dimensional plane, that is, a world of no restrictions at all, no boundaries, no limitation, no solids, no personalities, and very soon he felt very calm, greatly uplifted and filled with wonderful light.

Those heavy chains which bound his feet were now like simple strings to him, and quickly they snapped apart. Standing upright, he found the guards so sound asleep in their sense of materiality that they never noticed him moving toward the great iron door, which obediently opened to him of its own accord. And Peter, filled with the joy and marvel of wonderful Life, walked right out, free as the air.

"In the latter days I will pour out my Spirit upon all flesh." The Spirit, or Word, that man is a free, perfect, irresistible being, is now sweeping the universe. Heavenly realities are transcending human laws and material beliefs, for earth is to become heaven. Mortals will become immortals.

Time will become instantaneity. Darkness will become light. Night will become day. The desert will blossom as the rose, and the parched grounds will be streams of sparkling, flowing water. Even the ferocious lion will be gentle as the lamb and spiritual consciousness, like radiant light, will shine resplendent over all.

SELF-HARMONY

Self-harmony is that state of mind that is quiet, restful, confident; that does not reap its peace from the without but from the within. It is to maintain unruffled calm when you are blamed, abused or treated unjustly. It is to be habitually honest, upright, fearless, joyous, generous, loving and kind; to wonder at nothing that is said about you; to feel nothing that is done against you. It is perpetual calmness of thought based upon the conviction that the good alone is the all of life; it is to think nothing but good; to feel nothing but good; to act nothing but good. It is to have a joy so great that sorrow and hurt cannot pierce it; to have a soul so big, so full of love and compassion, that all who come within your mental touch will be strengthened, blessed and enriched. It is never to wound another by thought or act, but always to seek to cultivate and to unfold the good in those who are willing to be helped and enlightened.

True Identification

Part I

We are now living in the third dispensation, or revelation, of God to His people. The first dispensation was called "God the Father." In the Old Testament, God came to His people through His prophets, presenting truth to them, but only a few would listen. The second dispensation was called "God the Son." In the New Testament, we read of God coming to His people in the form of Jesus Christ, illustrating and personifying to them the real and true estate of man, but neither would humanity as a whole accept this revelation. Now, in the third and final dispensation, God comes to man as "God the Holy Ghost." God as Spirit reveals Himself in the heart of man, convincingly making known to him the absolute truth of his Being.

"The Comforter, which is the Holy Ghost, whom the Father will send in his name, he shall teach you all things, and bring all things to your remembrance, whatsoever I have said unto you" (John 14:26). "Look unto me, all the ends of the earth and be ye saved, for *I* am God, and besides me there is none else" (Isa. 45:22).

This is the voice of God, eternally speaking to His own people. Right here, it needs to be shown and explained how it is that God's people went astray and left Him, as it were. Apparently they left the kingdom of heavenly glory and abundance in which they lived and found themselves separated from Him — in want and in lack.

This idea of "the fall of man" is not taught in Christian Science. Mrs. Eddy gives no explanation of this subject or any elucidation but states plainly: "Mortals are not fallen children of God. They never had a perfect state of being which may subsequently be regained" (*Science and Health*, p. 476:13).

Nevertheless, this statement contradicts the Bible; contradicts also her other statements on this subject, for in the same text book she says: "Mortals will someday assert their freedom in the name of Almighty God" (p. 228:12) and "Mortals must gravitate Godward" (p. 265:5).

Now, in order to have you clearly perceive and understand what is called "the fall of man," I will show you an illustration, for without illustrations one is left with abstract reasoning which is purely intellectual. As the Bible tells us: "It is the Spirit that quickeneth" — it is the spirit of the thing which is the revelation; the words of themselves are mechanical. "The letter killeth, but the Spirit giveth life." We will now take up the illustration which will show you the perfect state of being as it was "in the beginning"; then how the separation began, in belief; and how finally man is to be reinstated in his original estate of perfection.

We will take for consideration a book, its author and its characters. For instance, several years ago I wrote a novel called *Glad Tidings*. In this book the heroine was called "Gloria Gilman." I created her. I was her life and being. She was nothing in and of herself.

Can you see this clearly? She represented me and my thoughts. When she spoke certain words in the book, it was always I, the author, speaking through her, magnifying myself. I gave her parents; I gave her opportunities wherein to enjoy herself. Everything she has of beauty, harmony, joy and delight, I, the author, furnished.

She manifested me. She could do *nothing* herself. She was my reflection! That is, in a state of meditation this book came forth, together with its characters. It was wholly my reflection. It expressed me, the author; it was one with me, verily, it was "me," I, the author. The author was unseen, invisible to the reader as the author, yet seen and made visible by and through characters.

It was I, the author, who created the trees, the animals, the water, the land and all the scenery in the book. It was I who did all the thinking, the planning and the feeling of everything in the book. All expression was myself expressed. I gave the characters names which I selected for them. and I brought them happiness and harmony according to my own ideas of rightness.

Now, in this particular book, called *Glad Tidings*, the heroine was called "Gloria Gilman"; but can you tell what was her real name? Can you see that her real name was "Lillian DeWaters"? It was surely none other. In the book, this character had parents—but who really made and created her? Lillian DeWaters. Gloria had no age or parents of her own. She did not live in a certain town or city as it appeared. She lived only in the author. Thus, in this sense, she was the author! And the author, Lillian DeWaters, was Gloria Gilman! They were one, and this one was Lillian DeWaters. The author, Lillian DeWaters, was the book and all its characters—all moving in one synchronization.

We now turn our attention to God, the real and only Creator of us and of all living things—the First, the Original, the Supreme, verily, the author of the Book of Life including all its characters. The perfect state of the Author and His characters, that is, the original state of Being and its characterization, was exactly the same as that of the author and her book as illustrated above. The characters in God's Book of Life had no mind, life, body, parents, children, age, habits or ideas of their own: they were the Author reflected—or reflections of God, the Author. These characters acted, as it were, as on a stage, every one having a certain work to do, certain parts to take, yet all reflecting the Author of the play, all operating as one Mind, one Life, one Being.

Now, the Bible informs us that the Author wrote into His story: "Choose ye whom ye will serve" (Josh. 24:15). Why? Because He wanted His characters to worship and love Him of their own free will. He gave them the right of choice—the freedom to love and to be, to act and to serve Him only. The Bible tells, however, that these characters chose not to worship their Creator, nor willingly and freely be His reflection, but they partook "of the knowledge of good and evil": they began to think for themselves, to create for themselves, to have children of their own, laws of their own, schools, churches, hospitals and cemeteries of their own: and naturally they began to find themselves in all kinds of troubles, dangers, and problems.

This "mist" or separation was never a real one, but was like a sleep, wherein things appear in dreams which are not true at all; which have no substance, no body, no life, no reality, no action, no being whatsoever; nevertheless, they give the feeling of fear, suffering and disquietude. This "sleep," mentioned early in Genesis and spoken of by Jesus and the apostles, is like the darkness which arises, naturally, where there is no light. The characters, typified by "Adam and Eve," partaking of the knowledge of both good and evil, found themselves in a darkened sense, or sleep; which darkness or sleep will never wholly vanish from man until he returns to the original state— God's reflection, or God, Himself, in manifestation.

When we are without light, we experience what is termed "darkness." It is no substance; it is a lack of substance; it is nothing. Similarly, when the characters refused to let the mind of their Author control and actuate them, automatically the light or understanding discontinued for them, and they found themselves in a state of darkness called, in the Book, a "sleep" or "mist" or "dream." It is nothing really. As a man on his bed, dreaming, never actually leaves his room, but only thinks he does, and experiences his false belief, so the characters, having turned from the wakeful, Christ state, or state of light and understanding, entered a "sleep," which, while it has no reality or truth in it, yet is of sufficient importance that God, the Author, from that time to this, has never ceased His aim to waken these characters and bring them back to the conscious awareness of their perfect state—and to do this through love and love alone.

I have loved thee with an everlasting love; therefore with loving kindness have I drawn thee (Jer. 31:3).

They have chosen their own ways, and their soul delighteth in their abomination (Isa. 66:3).

Because when I called, ye did not answer; when I spake, ye did not hear; but did evil before mine eyes, and did choose that wherein I delighted not (Isa. 65:12).

Is not my way equal? Are not your ways unequal? Cast away from you all your transgressions, whereby ye have transgressed (Ezek. 18:25, 31).

Verily, the veil, or covering, or mist, or dream, means the one thing—the character turning from his Author and thereby automatically feeling the sense of separation and darkness; and such will vanish only when the character returns to his Creator, willingly and lovingly letting God be his Mind, his Life, his Body, verily his All-in-All.

In the metaphysical field, it would seem that the characters are trying through their own "right thoughts" to waken themselves and bring themselves into their true position through these means. The characters (called mankind, humanity, mortals) cannot, in and of their personal selves, ever restore their perfect state of Being. This state they have never really lost or left; they have, however, lost sight of it, and it will come again into experience as they are willing to give up believing that they have a personal mind which thinks, and *let* that mind which was in Christ Jesus—God's mind, or God, think for them.

Then the character shall be the reflection or expression of God, and not a prodigal, dreaming that he is living in a material world of trouble, limitation, etc.; that is, he will be the manifestation here and now on earth. The thinking of right thoughts, no doubt, helps the character to do better dreaming, or to have a more harmonious experience in the dream: but only the letting go of the personal thinking so that the mind of God may be heard and accepted, will ever completely satisfy and deliver man, and cause him to awaken and remain awake, and actually and consciously be God, in manifestation.

"Take ye no (personal) thought," and then God, the one Mind, will do the thinking for you, and you, as the character in the Book of Life, will experience and express this true thinking automatically. Characters who believe that they have a mind of their own and that their joy consists in having "a free will" must finally be convinced, either through suffering or truth, that all such belief is futile. It has death as its objective, leading always away from God into darkness.

Who, then, is the sleeper or dreamer spoken of in the Bible and in metaphysical books of today? He may be you or I or anyone who is not aware of the real state of Being, wherein the character is not only a character, but he is, likewise, the Author! Does the Christ-man sleep or dream? No. He is our Self in our wakeful or true-knowing state. The wakeful man is not asleep; but if man does not live or act in his wakeful or knowing state, then he automatically partakes of the "mist" and becomes, as Jesus said, a prodigal, until he is willing to leave that position and take the steps back to his original and perfect state. In fact, this was Jesus' mission here on earth—to waken man from his dream by telling him and showing him the truth about himself, that God and man are one! In proportion as man believes this fact and turns from the dream of matter and mind, sin, disease and limitations, he will awaken and find himself in a universe of beauty and glory, of eternal love and harmony.

The Living Presence

Part II

I am the Light and the Truth; in Me is no darkness. *I* am Spirit; in Me is no matter. *I* am eternity; in Me is no age. *I* am infinity; in Me is no limitation. *I* am Presence; in Me is no absence of the actual experience of All-good, here and now.

What one now needs to see and emphasize is the presence of God in our midst. We must advance from the mental position or conception of God, that is, from the viewpoint of God as invisible Mind or Spirit, to the perception and conception of God as Presence — as a living actuality in our midst.

Where God is Presence, there is plenty; there is no lack. Where God is Presence there is health; there is no sickness or suffering. Where God is Presence, there is happiness; there is no grief or sorrow whatsoever. Therefore, bring your conscious knowing and living into subjection to the Christ, to the actual presence of God. Consider the *living* of the truth of greater importance than the mere talking it as repetition from a book. Actions speak louder than words; therefore begin to live and to act as really one with divine Love and Truth. Bringing your life, your actions and your emotions into subjection and harmony with the Christ, or your true Self, you will naturally manifest and express loving kindness to everyone, likewise meekness, simplicity, and loving understanding. Never will you feel or express criticism, dominance, condemnation or censure. Never will you uphold personality, but only the actual Presence in your midst.

As one thus advances from the purely mental concept, the intellectual or theoretical acceptance of truth to the practice and the living of it, his mind is automatically in subjection to the Christ; nay, more, he will have no mind of his own, for the Christ-mind will operate in him, and naturally, he will spontaneously show forth the very presence of God.

Besides surrendering the mind to God, one must also surrender the body to the real and the true. He must live so that his body is kept in a state of purity and chastity; he must therefore relinquish personal worship, human love, passion and appetite.

"They that are in the flesh cannot please God." They who experience the physical reaction or emotion which resentment, criticism, hatred, jealousy, pride, passion or lust bring are not experiencing the divine Presence. Paul continues in his eighth chapter to the Romans: "Ye are not in the flesh but in the Spirit, if so be that the Spirit of God dwells in you."

This is indeed the redemption of the body; through our willingness to live the truth in our body as well as in our thought, through our actions and emotions as well as through our thinking and speaking, we shall know that we are manifesting the Presence instead of "the flesh," or the fleshly or mortal concept of body.

Thus, as one lovingly, gladly and obediently lives the truth in action and in expression, he will be manifesting, to some degree, the "I AM" Presence, here and now. In many books of metaphysics and psychology it is stressed that we should give consideration mainly to our thinking, or to the spiritualization of our thoughts; but I say unto you, "Take ye no thought" what ye shall think, but instead consider how you are speaking, acting and feeling, and to what extent you are bringing into outer expression and visibility the very presence of Truth. If you are honest and sincere and your aim and your intense spiritual desire is to live and act and be the life of Spirit here and now, " *I* am with you, even unto the end of the (dream) world."

We are all living, here on earth, in the very presence of God, but not all are conscious of it. We do not need to bring God upon earth, but we do need to surrender our minds and our bodies for His divine mind and perfect body that we shall be able to behold Him, for, "… when He shall appear (to us) we shall be like Him, for we shall see Him as He is" (1 John 3:2). By harmonizing our lives with His will and by bringing our feelings and our emotions into harmony with His law, we shall come naturally into the experience of the abundance of all good, according to His promise: "Blessed are the pure in heart: for they shall see (and experience) God."

Living the life of Truth in our hearts, we gladly "renounce the hidden things of dishonesty, not walking in craftiness, nor handling the word of God deceitfully; but by manifestation of the truth" (2 Cor. 4:2). God then rules in us and over us, and our whole life is under His care and jurisdiction. Thus, His mind is enthroned in us and His body is expressed by us; truly we are His and He is ours and we can truthfully say, "I and my Father are one."

The experience of good will come to us and will be evidenced more and more in our body and in our affairs as we take God from the mental realm of thinking and bring Him before us as an actual presence.

In metaphysics God is considered as Mind, or an invisible substance; but to confine one's concept of God to that of invisible mind or Spirit is to deprive oneself of the fuller revelation that God is an actual living Presence in our midst, that is, God is a visible reality or presence.

It is indeed wonderful to be able to rise from the view that God is wholly Mind, or invisible Principle, to that of God as a tangible Presence. Holding to God as Mind or Principle tends to keep God in the mental realm, that is, tends to keep God invisible, but opening our vision to fuller revelation, we behold that God is likewise visible, that God is present as manifested form.

God is in all, overall, and in you all and, "By him all things consist" (Col. 1:16). "What? Know ye not that your body is the temple of the Holy Ghost which is in you, and ye are not your own? Glorify God in your body and in your Spirit, which are God's" (1 Cor. 6:19-20).

Therefore, instead of believing or thinking of your body as "mortal" or "matter" or "human," one may, if he will but be receptive and open his vision, see and understand that his body is not his own but is the body of God!

There are no individual bodies to be governed by individual minds! This is the view of those who do not or will not see beyond it; but the great fact eternally exists to be revealed to those who are ready to accept it, that there is but one body only—the body of God, the Creator. God is here, there, everywhere. By Him all things consist. God visualizes Himself as light, air, beauty, music, as well as all the loveliness of nature; likewise, as all formation—the form of bird, beast, man.

Verily, when we shall be willing to bring our hearts and our lives into harmony with God, then shall we begin to see God in manifested form before us. As our bodies are His temple, necessarily He will be present in His temple when we make this wonder possible. In proportion as we become pure in heart, will He reveal Himself to us; and in proportion as we live the true life here and now will He abide within us, and no longer shall we be "mortal," "material" or "human beings," but we shall know that God is the only Presence—that "I and my Father are one."

If one considers God only as in the mental realm, that is, if one associates God with "Mind" only, then only there can he find Him; but when one has received the fuller revelation that God is manifested as visible presence, living form, then he will find God manifested in his body and in his affairs. We have heard it said that we should not try to spiritualize matter. This is correct. Nor could such a thing be done, when there is no matter! When it is truly seen that "by him all things consist," then one will be willing to cease believing that his body is matter; he will moreover cease thinking and speaking of "matter" altogether, and the word will become obsolete to him.

Are you willing to understand that "there is no matter," and hence no material body, for "by him all things consist"? Furthermore, do you know that "By him were all things created, that are in heaven and that are in earth visible and invisible, all things were created by him and for Him?" (Col. 1:16). If so, then will you begin today to regard your body as the work of God, hence good and perfect, immutable, indestructible, immortal and incorruptible? And will you forever cease thinking of the body as a human concept, as one with mortal thought, or as material or mortal? It is indeed glorious to bring God so near to one as to see that He is not only one's mind but that He is also one's body! That He is actually a living, present all-inclusive reality!

Not only must one relinquish his belief that he has an individual mind, but moreover that he has an individual body. Such relinquishment for the actual presence of God here and now is indeed the "redemption of the body" to which Paul refers. What can redeem the body from sickness, disease, suffering and death but the truth that God is body as well as mind! God is the visible as well as the invisible! God is here as well as the hereafter! God is the Word made flesh, and dwells among us!

As one redeems his concept of mind, by seeing that there is but one mind—the mind of God—so must one also redeem his concept of body by seeing that there is but one body—the body of God; that all forms are truly as spiritual as the God who made them. To him of spiritual vision, of receptive, willing heart, God is the manifest as well as the unmanifest, the visible as well as the invisible; God is body as well as Soul.

Jesus, who was the Word made flesh, who was verily Emmanuel, or God with us, did surely personify God, and so shall we all be able to do likewise in proportion as we are able to lose our sense of an individual mind and body and behold God as He is—All-in-All! This, of course, we cannot do, nor can we see God as a living presence among us while we think in words and ideas other than the real and true ones. With the conviction of one mind, one power, one body, one presence, and with the earnest and willing desire to live and to embody this truth here and now, we shall make great strides toward seeing Him as He is, and consequently being like Him.

As we see God, the Word, in the flesh, or in visible form, as well as in mind, or the mental realm, we shall be harmonizing ourselves with

Him in the without as well as in the within. It should be seen and understood that an author of a book is not only the invisible intelligence, but that he is also the tangible characters! It is truly a great light to see that God, the author of the Book of Life, includes all His characters. They are all the offspring of His mind, and in them He lives, moves, and enacts His presence, power and being. They are nothing of themselves; they are Himself. He in them, and they in Him; the invisible made visible, and the true mental made an actual, living Presence.

Therefore "Glorify God in your body, and in your spirit, which are God's." Give God not only your mind, but give Him also your body, so that not only will His mind be your mind, but His body will be your body. Thus shall your mind and your body be redeemed, and as it reads in Isaiah, "Instead of the thorn shall come up the fir tree, and instead of the briar shall come up the myrtle tree."

Likewise, instead of the mortal, material body—the body representing the beliefs of birth, age and death, there will come up, or be seen, the spiritual body of life, light and love—the body of the Resurrection. Thus shall God live with men and walk in them, and we shall not only be the characters in the Book of Life, but we shall know that we are also the author. I AM THAT I AM is the *only* Presence.

Treatment

Part III

God's work is finished, and He pronounced it "very good." Moreover, "as it was in the beginning, it is now, and ever shall be, world without end." Nothing can be taken from nor added to God's perfect, finished work. I therefore accept it as it is. I praise and glorify God because of it; and I acknowledge His immaculately perfect creation as existing here and now.

God, the I AM, is always supplying and supporting His perfect world, perfectly and abundantly. As a character, I am included in His world.

There is but one Creator, God, and but one creation, His workmanship. This one creation, including man and all living things, is perfect and present now, awaiting our individual recognition and claim, in order that we, as characters in His Book of Life, may "see Him as He is," and thus "be like Him" —even to sense and sight.

God creates all forms of reality. As these forms express Him, they necessarily must express perpetual and changeless harmony, beauty, action, order, life and health. The fullness and abundance of God's ideas and their corresponding forms is present and available for all, here and now, who acknowledge and accept them.

The body of man, beast and every living thing is governed and controlled by God, the one and only maker and creator of them. Therefore I give unto God the glory due unto His glorious name; I rejoice in Him, love and trust Him with all my heart, and surely He will abundantly and all-triumphantly bring all-good to pass in my experience.

God not only comprises and includes spiritual ideas, but their forms as well. And we shall see these true and perfect forms about us as we recognize and accept this fact as true, and as we live more and more consistent with our spiritual vision and understanding:

"I am the Lord; that is my name; and my glory will I not give to another." Hear, therefore, my people, and understand. Creation is not mortal nor material, neither is the body matter. Moreover, no mind exists but the I AM. It is for you, the characters, to see and accept this glorious fact of being and cease giving power to aught but Me.

Acknowledge no mind but My mind. Acknowledge no power but My power. Acknowledge no body but My body. Acknowledge no being but My being — the I AM THAT I AM, for "I am God; and besides me, there is none else."

I am all action, function and form. All things were made by Me; and without Me was not anything made that was made. My action is ever-present, constant and uninterrupted. My function is perfect, harmonious and impeccable. My form is My body, My universe, My creation.

Nothing can stop, stay or hinder My perfect action, feeling, function and form. *I* am the one and only power, actor and expressor. *I* am likewise the one and only formation, action, body and world. Besides Me and My power, truly there is none else.

Thus as characters in His Book of Life, we are perfect, glorious, divine, for we have His mind, His life, His action and His body. By putting aside all opposite and contrary teaching and beliefs, and by acknowledging and claiming these absolute and true facts of Being, we shall gradually waken as from sleep, and exclaim in ecstasy as did Jesus. "I and My Father are one."

"BY GRACE ARE YE SAVED"

By grace are ye saved through faith; and not of yourselves. It is the gift of God; for we are His workmanship, created in Christ Jesus (Eph. 2:8,10).

"Grace" means the act of God—the I AM THAT I AM. Grace has nothing to do with the works of the individual, what he does or does not do in the dream. Already, and before he takes any action whatever, man (in his real position), is God manifested, even as characters in a book of fiction are nothing of themselves but are the author. One has, therefore, to see and know this truth.

We are not obliged to save ourselves, nor bring about by our own personal efforts peace, health, harmony and the abundance of all good on earth, as though they were not eternally existent, but we are commanded to, "Turn unto Me! Accept Me!" That is, we should stop trying to fix over and correct the world seemingly external to us, and instead we should begin to understand who we really are, and then consciously accept this perfect God—praising Him, loving Him, rejoicing in Him, and yielding ourselves entirely to Him. The redeemed world will then take place automatically.

Today, we see mankind attempting to change the world from evil to good, from lack to abundance and from war to peace, believing that this is the right way to establish peace on earth. But this act of man will never bring forth the correct answer, nor will it ever achieve the goal he wishes, and which is rightfully his. Why? Because he is unaware of the fact that the kingdom of heaven is already at hand and that he is to be delivered and saved from evil through grace — through and by accepting and complying with the demands of God, namely, turn unto Me; believe in Me, praise Me, reduce your personal self to nothing that *I* may be all of you!

Man, in turning to the world and in trying to correct it, in turning to other human beings and in attempting to educate and better them, is forgetful and unmindful of the eternal fact that *by grace are ye saved.*

Ye are already saved! The kingdom of eternal wonder and glory and peace and abundance is already at hand. God has already created and finished His perfect work, including you and the world. But you, as individual being, will not fully experience and enjoy this heaven in which you live until you become wakeful and mindful of these true facts and begin to live the life of Spirit.

Man's sense of separation came about in the first place because he wanted to be something or somebody "of himself," and because he chose to turn from the "Garden of Eden," or the conscious state of abundance of all-good, for a taste of personality — personal aims, personal likes and dislikes. In this disobedient state of consciousness he found (and still finds today) impermanence, limitation, tribulation and defeat. His world is an imaginative world induced by his own sleep. Nor will he be able to again experience the heavenly world in which God placed him, until he sees his mistake, turns from it and attempts to wake up.

With his awakening will come the automatic restoration, the same as upon awakening from his night sleep, one is laborlessly restored to the consciousness of his bedroom. By grace he is already in his bedroom, safe and secure, but in his sleep he may dream that he is not in his home at all, but on the contrary, is living in another place where he is subjected to great fear and trouble. The perfect escape from any sleeping dream is to awaken. Likewise, in this world wherein there seem to be vicissitudes, dangers, troubles, sin, sickness and death, the perfect escape is for man to be willing to give up the struggle to create happiness, harmony and success by his own personal efforts, and have faith in God and His perfect creation.

God came into the dream-world, where sin, sickness and all kinds of evil seem to abound; He came in the body called Jesus Christ, to show to humanity, or the prodigal son, his true estate of being, that is, man's real, genuine state when he is awake; and the Bible states that all who accept Jesus Christ are saved and delivered; all who see and accept that their real state is not that of a human man at all, but instead is God manifested, are saved from the mortal dream. This promise is as true today as when it was uttered. Turning away from the false to the true and holding steadfastly to what is so, will absolutely waken us and will automatically deliver us from the unhappy dream-conditions of limitations of every name and nature.

As we take our true position as the Son of God, or God, the Son—that is, God manifested—the false beliefs will fade away, and the dream of material existence will begin to vanish. When we are willing to become pure in heart, then shall we understand that our concern is not with the world and its evil, but with ourselves and our own beliefs. If this were not so, then indeed would man never know that "by grace are ye saved." To be spiritually minded is life eternal. To let Spirit reflect Itself in us is to manifest God, or Christ, here and now; but this true state cannot be experienced while man is attempting to create a world for himself or personally make over his body and his affairs.

The eternal command of Jesus to us all is, "Be ye therefore perfect." How can a human being be perfect? He cannot. He cannot, of himself, be perfect, but he can accept the perfection which has already been bestowed upon him. Human beings, or beings such as we find ourselves today, can and must eventually turn from the material sense of existence to God and accept His perfection as our own being. We will then find ourselves in heaven, and the false material sense will have vanished.

In turning from the false view to the true perception, we must willingly part with sin — in disposition and action. We should watch well how we react to people, circumstances and things: for the inner emotion of resentment, confusion, disturbance, ill-will and such like, show us what work is needed to be done in our own consciousness. Paul plainly tells about the "works of the flesh," in his letter to the Galatians, 5th chapter: "But if ye bite and devour one another, take heed that ye be not consumed one of the other."

When we react with inner discordant emotion to the disposition, words or acts of another, we can feel certain that we need to bring more purity into our own consciousness. Let us ask ourself frequently, "How much do I love God?" For if we really love God enough, we will gladly and willingly turn away from the claims of personality — the purely human affections, passions and emotions, and maintain a calm which is undisturbed by thoughts, words or feelings of another. Such tests come to us daily, and great is our reward when we are able to say with the spiritually minded Paul, "None of these things move me!"

Many people find themselves suffering because of the sins of others, at least so they say and think. Yet this is never true. One suffers only for his own shortcomings, even if he allows himself to suffer, as he believes, because of the faults of another. There is scarcely a family today but what in its midst are those who grieve and suffer because certain loved ones seem to be in trouble of some kind. Such sympathetic suffering, while seemingly humanly impossible to resist, is nevertheless controllable when one turns to God. It is wrong to suffer for the sins of another. God does not ask it of us. A mother may say that because her son is not willing to live the life of temperance, "He is killing me." But such is not true. As she turns herself to God in full surrender of herself and of her son, she will find her spiritual peace and harmony, and the son, too, will feel the spiritual effect.

Allowing oneself to believe that his state of health or harmony is at the mercy of another is darkness. We are each, whether we know it or not, a law unto ourself. If we let others make us unhappy, then no one is to blame but ourself; for there is a way in which we can turn to God, and loving Him supremely, leave all with Him and feel and experience the rest and peace of heaven. To help another is right, but to allow that other to darken our spiritual sense is wrong. To help another, we can say quietly and mentally to him: "Because you are the Son of God, or God manifested, then you are temperate, sincere, pure, honest and good; I praise God that this is the way you are now and here, and you are no other way!" Love this fact and believe it with your whole heart and soul. It is the truth.

As the lesson of self-control, which is really to be God-controlled, is learned and practiced, one begins to find a lovely peace and poise which is natural and unaffected. Loving God supremely causes us to desire willingly and earnestly to keep His commandments. He says, "Love thy neighbor as thyself." We can surely do this, not sympathetically or humanly, but with spiritual vision. Turning from the false presentation another is showing and exhibiting, through his disposition and manner, words and actions, to the spiritual part of him, or his real wakeful state, and rejoicing in the presence of that, we can be undisturbed by the dream he presents to us. First of all we are to *conquer ourself*, even as Paul says, and in this way only can we feel and know the love and peace, the glory and satisfaction which come to us through our obedience to the heavenly law.

Purifying ourselves thus, our lives take on new tones and characteristics, and more and more we personify the God-man—God Himself in manifested form.

Said Jesus, "The truth shall make you free." Whom? You! Not the human mind, but you— God's man. The Truth will free you from your false beliefs. The Truth will waken you from darkness and sleep, if you will let It! Nor does the Author write the "sleep" or the "dream" into His Book of Life. He writes only reality. He does not write evil of any kind, nor sickness, sorrow or death. It is man who dreams such things because he has turned away from God, his Author. Thus, the admonition is given, "Turn every man from his evil way" Jer. 26:3). Ever calls the Author: "Come unto Me!" Turn from your transgressions! "Awake, thou, that sleepest!"

You shall know the truth! Who? You and I. We are the ones Jesus meant. Man shall know the truth. What man? God's man. What other man is there who could know the truth? Strange that many have not seen this fact before, but still hold to the outgrown theory and false belief that it is some man other than God's man who is to know the truth and enter into his original freedom. "Cease ye from man, whose breath is in his nostrils, for wherein is he to be accounted of!" (Isa. 2:22). The only man we can account for is God's man. He is the one Jesus came to save and to awaken. Is this not so? Are we not God's man, and are we not the very ones who must turn to God for revelation, salvation and deliverance? To be sure. "Put off the old man and put ye on the new man, which after God is created in righteousness and true holiness" (Eph. 4:32-34). Who is it that is to "put off the old man?" It is you and I. Who is it that is to "put on the new man?" It is you and I. We are to stop thinking, acting and feeling contrary to the Christ, and we are to return to our Father's house, the consciousness of our true being as one with God, hence inherently and innately righteous and perfect.

In knowing and accepting the truth that God is the only mind and is therefore our mind, and that God is the only body and is therefore our body, and that we never had another except as in a dream, which is really nothing whatever, we shall set ourselves free from the "far country" and will find ourselves reinstated in our original position of man in the likeness of God.

Therefore you need no longer seek into books to discover who it is that is the false believer or who it is that dreams. Have not we all entertained false beliefs? Surely, we have. Very well, then, in this sense, we are the sleepers and dreamers. Have not we all believed that we were sick, in pain, trouble and sorrow? Surely we have. Do you not now believe it to be impossible for you to walk on the water? To pass through closed doors? To become invisible and again visible? Certainly you do. And so do I. Well, these are false beliefs, for if we knew how, we could surely do these very things now and here: we are made capable of doing them.

Verily the sleeper is not the human mind, nor the race belief, nor the universal consciousness, nor even mortal mind, but the sleeper is man himself. The Bible, both in the Old and the New Testament, tells us so. "Ye must be born again." Who? Man, who is really the Son of God, though unaware of it or not fully conscious of it. Why did Jesus come on earth? To set men free from the curse of their false beliefs. "I am come a light into the world, that whosoever believeth in me should not abide in darkness" (John 12:46). Jesus continued in the verse following: "I am come to save the world." Furthermore, he said "I am come that they might have life, and have it more abundantly." Who? God's man and none other. Do you not admit that you are God's man? And do you not also admit that you desire to be enlightened and to enjoy life more abundantly? Certainly, you do.

Turn your attention to the story of the prodigal son. Who was this son? He was the son of a certain rich man. Whom does this rich man illustrate? God, the Father of us all. Was not this prodigal the rich man's son even while he lived in the far country? Certainly. Living in the midst of degradation and deprivation did not change whatsoever the relationship between this father and his son. No matter where the son was, nor what he was doing, all the time he was the "father's" son. And Jesus showed that all the son needed in order to enjoy and consciously partake of the father's abundance was to leave the far country and return home.

Verily, we are the Sons of God right here on earth today! No matter how far we have seemed to wander into the beliefs of sin and suffering, still our relationship to God, our Father, has never changed. He loves us "with an everlasting love." Neither false beliefs, nor dreams, nor darkness, nor ignorance, nor childish things, nor powers, nor things present, nor things to come shall be able to separate us from our Creator nor cause us to be other than who we are—the reflection of our Author, or God manifested.

Jesus came into the world to free us, God's children, or characters in His own Book of Life. Who can doubt this to be true when he reads in John's gospel, the first chapter: "He came unto his own, and his own received him not." It would be impossible to misinterpret these words. "Jesus came into the world to save sinners; of whom I am chief." Thus spoke Paul, the great evangelist. Is a sinner God's child, or character? Most certainly. The prodigal son typified the sinner; yet even in his sin, or mistake, he was ever the rich man's son.

It must be seen that *a dream has no truth in it!* A dream is not a reality; a dream is an unreality. Man has never lost himself, nor actually separated himself from God, his Author: he has only lost sight of himself as perfect, and of his perfect world, but by knowing the truth, he will waken from his "sleep" and find the eternal order remaining unchanged.

The Bible is our perfect teacher. It tells us plainly that Jesus "came unto his own ... and to as many as received him, to them gave he power to become (on earth, here and now) the Sons of

God." Jesus came to his own people because he loved them—not that they were really lost or "fallen," but that they had lost sight of their own perfection as, in and of God, their Creator; and because they had fallen into a "sleep" from which he could easily waken them.

Behold, the tabernacle of God is with men, and he will dwell with them, and they shall be His people, and God Himself shall be with them, and be their God. And God shall wipe away all tears from their eyes: and there shall be no more death, neither sorrow, nor crying, neither shall there be any more pain: for the former things are passed away .... He (God's child, or character) that overcometh (false belief) shall inherit all things: and I will be his God, and he shall be my son. (Rev. 21: 3-4, 7)

THE TRUE CONCEPT

"God created heaven, and the things that therein are, and the earth, and the things that therein are" (Rev. 10:6).

"I have made the earth, and created man upon it; I, even my hands, have stretched out the heavens, and all their host have I commanded" (Isa. 45:12).

"Have we not all one Father? Hath not one God created us?" (Mal.2:10).

"In the beginning God created the heavens and the earth ... and God made the beast of the earth after his kind, and the cattle after their kind: and God saw that it was good. And God said, Let us make man in our own image, after our likeness; and let them have dominion over the fish of the sea, and over the fowl of the air ... and over every creeping thing that creepeth upon the earth. And God created man in his own likeness; in the image of God created He him; male and female created he them (Gen. 1:1, 25-27).

"All things were made by him, and without him was not anything made that was made" (John 1:3).

I AM THAT I AM is the perfection of all things. *I am the kingdom of heaven, the manifested Perfection. I am the substance of all formation. I am the fullness and the abundance of all good.* "This then is the message which we have heard of him, and declared unto you, that God is light, and in him is no darkness at all" (1 John 1:5). There can be no darkness, such as sickness, disorder or lack of harmony in My presence. There can be no formation of disease, nor any presence of evil in My kingdom: besides Me, there is none else.

"I know that whatsoever God doeth, it shall be forever; nothing can be put to it, nor anything taken from it" (Eccles. 3:14). Therefore, we are saved already because of our inherent and innate oneness with God; and nothing can keep us from the conscious realization and experience of this perfection, harmony and completeness if we turn from the false seeming to the true state and accept and embody it.

But we must take the steps out of ignorance into understanding; out of darkness into light. "When I became a man, I put away childish things" (1 Cor. 13:11) "because the darkness is past, and the true light now shineth" (1 John 2:8). Therefore, we must gladly and willingly leave the childish position of seeing and speaking about mortal mind and the human mind as power or cause of evil and advance to the perception that God is our mind and we never had another; God is also our body, and we have had no other. We should not fear in letting go the childish notion of matter and human mind as we advance into the revelation and acknowledgment of one mind and one body, all-inclusive. The words *matter, mortal mind,* and *human mind* should become obsolete to us.

In metaphysics, we read much about spiritualizing, correcting and educating the human mind, or mortal mind. The time is here, now, to outgrow such statements and such beliefs. As understanding unfolds to us, we should advance in our language and expression. Now, who stands back of the "human mind" one talks about? He does. Therefore one is himself the creator of the belief in a human mind! Surely

God does not make it. Inasmuch as God is not its creator then man, in ignorance, makes and serves it by his recognition of it; but when one sees that the divine Mind is the only Mind which is cause, then will he be willing to let go the childish belief in the human mind as causation or as an entity which must be corrected or spiritualized.

We read in *Science and Health* by Mrs. Eddy that "Mortal mind is the criminal in every case." Now, which is first: man, or his belief in a mortal mind? It is man himself who has this concept of mortal mind. Indeed, it is quite as irrelevant to place the blame of one's misfortune upon the mortal mind as it would be to blame one's feet should they stumble upon a stone. When man is willing to see and admit that his trouble comes from not yielding himself wholly to God, learning of and obeying His requirements of him, as well as living up to his highest inspiration and revelation, he will then be in the right position to advance into greater light and understanding, and consequently, into greater harmony and abundance.

The conceiver always precedes his conceptions. Therefore man himself precedes his idea of mortal mind, or the human mind, does he not? "When that which is perfect is come, then that which is in part shall be done away" (1 Cor. 13:10).

Revelation of Truth is continually coming to man on earth. It was surely a great discovery or revelation to see that God is not responsible for any sickness, trouble or disaster on the face of this earth. This was truly a marvelous insight. It was also a revelation to discern that "Mortal mind is a solecism in language" (*Science and Health,* p.114:12) and that "this so-called mind is a myth." (p. 152:1). Therefore, to be true to this revelation we must give up the theory that we can translate or educate or spiritualize a myth! We can, however—nay, *we must*—educate and spiritualize our sense of things and change our own sense from the childish belief in mortal mind to the ripened understanding that there is no mind but God.

"God hath made man upright; but they have sought out many inventions" (Eccles. 7:29). Whom did God make "upright"? Man. Who was responsible for the inventions? Man—"they" themselves. The blame is not placed upon anything or anyone but upon man himself. The first mistake of man has been to place the cause of evil upon something outside himself: upon the devil, or mortal mind, or human mind, or upon the race consciousness or the universal belief. His next mistake has been in trying to change or correct the evil thing which he himself invented. Let man turn within, even as Jesus admonished. He will then find the kingdom of heaven (understanding) right at hand. See, accept, acknowledge and embody it, and the false beliefs which you are entertaining will fade away. "If you believe in and practice wrong knowingly, you can at once change your course and do right." (*Science and Health* p. 253:18). "Each individual is responsible for himself." (*Miscellaneous. Writings* p. 119:8). "Unwittingly you sentence yourself to suffer." *(Science and Health* p. 378: 4). These sentences correspond with Jesus' teaching that it is man himself, verily, God's man, who must awake and be redeemed; who must leave the far country and take the required steps back to his Father's house.

Truly, as we turn from ignorance to understanding and as we accept and embody these true facts of life and being, we shall rise into that new creature which the Bible promises in such glowing terms: "Put on the new man, which after God is created in righteousness and true holiness. Wherefore putting away lying, speak every man truth with his neighbor; for ye are members one of another" (Eph. 4:24-25).

"They which are the children of the flesh, these are not the children of God" (Rom. 9:8). They who believe that they are of the flesh, rather than children of God, are in ignorance. We are never actually mortals, but apparently [we believe] we are such. We cannot be children of understanding and believe otherwise than this.

Is man ever actually mortal or material? No. Can he believe otherwise? Yes. When Jesus raised Lazarus from the dead, for instance, and called to him, "Lazarus, come forth," did he call to the

Christ-man? No. Did he call to the human mind? No. To whom did Jesus speak? He spoke to God's man who, at that instant, was entertaining a false belief. This was the mission of Jesus: to lead or turn man back to the truth of his being.

"He came unto his own." He came, apparently, to the children of men, who were really the children of God. Can the Christ-man dream or have a false belief? No. He is the man awake in the conscious knowledge and expression of his genuine and true estate—the likeness of God. Are we the Christ-man now? Yes; but as Jesus said, we need to know this and to embody it.

What caused a dream or a false belief? Ignorance or lack of true understanding. What will restore us to the conscious expression of our inherent perfection? The acceptance of the truth and the living of it. Is there any growth or translation or change for us to acquire? "Grow in grace and in the knowledge of our Lord and Savior, Jesus Christ. To him be glory, both now and ever" (2 Peter 3:18). According to the New Testament, Jesus Christ is in us all, for Paul asked, "Know ye not that Jesus Christ is in you?" "He is our true, wakeful Self. He is the Self that we should recognize and claim as our genuine Being on earth as in heaven. We are actually this perfect Self now, and it is the perception, acceptance, realization, acknowledgment and embodiment of this fact that will waken us, stop the dream and set us free from the illusion.

The kingdom of heaven is here: we are now living in its presence. If we are not conscious of it, then let us partake of higher understanding and more unselfish love. Light, laughter, joy, peace and the glorious abundance and fullness of all-good, all are here. By grace this is so: thus, we have only to believe, accept, acknowledge and embody this wonderful and glorious revelation, freedom and liberty which God continually bestows upon us.

About the Author

Lillian DeWaters was born in 1883 and lived in Stamford Connecticut. She grew up with a Christian Science background and in her early teens began to study metaphysics and on that same day to seriously study the Bible. "It was from the Bible that I learned to turn from all else to God direct.... What stood out to me above all else was the fact presented, that when they turned to God they received Light and Revelation; they walked and talked with God; and they found peace and freedom."

She published several books while actively within the Christian Science organization and then in 1924 she had an awakening experience when it was as though a veil was parted and Truth was revealed to her. From that point she began to receive numerous unfoldments, and became a prolific writer.

She created her own publishing company and published over 30 books in 15 languages. She was a well-known teacher who taught regularly at the Waldorf Astoria in New York and she was sought after as a spiritual healer.

Each of her books was written based on direct unfoldments of Absolute Truth that serious students will immediately recognize and treasure.

Made in the USA
Las Vegas, NV
05 March 2024

86752689R00099